meet Me here

meet Me here

Bible Reading Methods to Know and Experience God

Kim-Christine Duarté

foreword by Scott Camp

RESOURCE *Publications* · Eugene, Oregon

MEET ME HERE
Bible Reading Methods to Know and Experience God

Resource Publications
An Imprint of Wipf and Stock Publishers
199 W. 8th Ave., Suite 3
Eugene, OR 97401

www.wipfandstock.com

PAPERBACK ISBN: 978-1-5326-8392-3
HARDCOVER ISBN: 978-1-5326-8393-0
EBOOK ISBN: 978-1-5326-8394-7

Manufactured in the U.S.A.   OCTOBER 10, 2019

For my loving and supportive husband, Zane,
and our sons, Isaiah and Zachary.

Isaiah and Zachary,

It is my hope, my prayer, that you would be dedicated in your pursuit of God through the in-depth reading of his Word and persistent prayer. May you know the joy of fulfilling your God-given purpose, making lifestyle choices and decisions out of your love and reverence for God. Remember, sons, life is short, so live for God.

With all my love,
Mom

CONTENTS

FOREWORD

ANYONE WHO HAS EVER picked up the Bible in an attempt to read with understanding knows firsthand the challenge of this endeavor. This simple and practical book is the perfect tool for the person, student, or church who desires to hear God's voice and experience his power through Scripture. In her book, Kim-Christine provides straightforward Bible reading approaches that will teach Christians how to read and engage the Bible for themselves.

The *K-I-N-G-S-!* *Method* is a step-by-step approach that teaches readers how to understand the author's intended meaning while emphasizing the importance of applying that message with the guidance of the Holy Spirit. This is a reliable approach for understanding the meaning of a passage and a powerful way to know God through his Word.

Also, to experience a meaningful devotional time, it's helpful to communicate with God through the Bible, allowing the Holy Spirit to reveal areas that need to be surrendered to him. I believe Kim-Christine's devotional approach accomplishes this crucial spiritual discipline.

Additionally, to grow spiritually, it's essential to spend time in God's presence consistently. In her book, Kim-Christine includes a program to help you or your church develop devotional habits through genuine fellowship.

This hands-on guide will better equip Christians and the church to understand passages, connect with God through Scripture, and become consistent in their daily walk with him. As a result, these spiritual disciplines will help individuals fulfill their God-given purpose. I welcome those who love to read the sacred text to employ Kim-Christine's Bible Study methods in your pursuit of understanding and applying God's Word to your lived experience.

Scott Camp

Evangelist, Author, Educator
Host of *The Conversation* Podcast

ACKNOWLEDGEMENTS

A SPECIAL THANK YOU to **Dr. John Wesley Wycoff**, my graduate professor of Hermeneutics at Southwestern Assemblies of God University in Waxahachie, Texas. Much of the content in this book, including the K-I-N-G-S-! Method, was gleaned from his lectures, class discussions, and assignments.

Also, a special thank you to **Debra Smith and Rachel Smith**, from D&R WordSmiths, for the in-depth professional editing of this book. https://www.drwordsmiths.com/

And, a heartfelt thanks to:

- God, my constant help, guide, and provider for this project. I love you.

- my husband and life-long love, Zane Duarté. This project has costed more time, energy, and resources than ever imagined. Thank you for your faithful love and support. And, thank you for allowing me to be transparent and share some of our stories. Also, thank you for coming up with the creative title for this book, *meet Me here*. I love you.

- my sons, Isaiah and Zachary Michael, who have been patient while I've spent countless hours working on this project. I love you, sons.

- my mom, Mary Otto, who has shown unconditional love and support throughout this project (and my life). And, thank you, Mike, for your support, too. I appreciate you both so very much.

- my loving and supportive siblings and family members: Adam and Trisha, Carrie, Lisa, Stacy, Elizabeth, and Timmy. I miss you, Lori. And, Carrie and Stacy, thank you for your helpful suggestions. I greatly appreciated your feedback. And thank you, Mom and Dad Duarte, for your love and support. You are greatly appreciated.

- Jean Carlson, my closest friend and prayer partner. I love you, sister. Thank you for being a steadfast friend. And, thank you, Phil and Jean, for your helpful feedback and suggestions! I am very grateful.

- John and Cindy Palmer, from Waco First Assembly of God and, Bobby and Penny Haney, from 1Twenty2 Ministries, for letting me share this material while it was still rough.

- Pastor Josh and Heather Morgan and my church family, from Connect4LIFE church, for your prayers and support.

INTRODUCTION

THIS BOOK WAS WRITTEN for *you* —the person, pastor, or the hands-on ministry student who desires to know God's truth and experience his presence through Scripture. That's why, in a simple and personal way, I provide three practical and specific ways to read the Bible that will help you do just that. The three methods are: 1) The K-I-N-G-S-! Method 2) the P-R-A-Y Devotional Bible Reading Method, and 3) the 4-P Bible Study Method.

The first approach, The K-I-N-G-S-! Method, is a step-by-step Bible study approach that focuses on understanding the meaning of a passage. Let's face it, there's a lot of confusion out there when it comes to understanding Scripture. But thankfully there are concrete guidelines for knowing the true meaning of a passage (a discipline called hermeneutics). Sadly, most people don't know these rules because they find it boring, or even hard, to learn.

That's why I have taken out the scholastic jargon and put the guidelines into simple steps using the acronym K-I-N-G-S-! Rest assured, friend, the concepts themselves are easy—and liberating—to learn. This book will show you how to understand the true meaning of a passage for yourself using the K-I-N-G-S-! step-by-step method (found in chapter 5).

The P-R-A-Y Method found in chapter 3 is a simple way to read the Bible devotionally to connect with God. Though it's necessary to understand the true meaning of a passage, it's also important to hear what God is speaking to us personally through it.

The steps in the P-R-A-Y Method encourage us to invite God into our hearts and minds to speak to us. In essence, this approach walks us through the Psalm 139:23–24 (NLT) prayer, "Search me, O God, and know my heart; test me and know my anxious thoughts. Point out anything in me that offends you, and lead me along the path of everlasting life."

The last method I share, the 4-P Bible Study Method found in chapter 4, is a mix between the two approaches. This is a simple Bible study method that can be done daily.

Then, in chapters 6–9 I share some simple tips for reading the different types of writing styles found in the Bible. I include helpful tips for reading biblical poetry, Old Testament genres, and New Testament genres.

I complete this Bible-reading guide by suggesting specific day-to-day practices for reading God's Word consistently (chapter 9). When we engage in God's word daily, it will help us know God better, discern his truth, and experience his power in our lives.

For your convenience, I include a Bible Reading Tools section. It contains the meet-Me-here Journey, a 40-day devotional kickoff, and a quick reference sheet for each of the three Bible-reading methods provided in this book.

It is my hope, my prayer, that after reading this guide, you will: 1) feel confident in your own ability to understand passages, 2) connect with God through Scripture, and 3) develop a consistent devotional life. That way you'll experience God's love for you and fulfill his purpose for your life.

With all my love,
Kim-Christine

How to Use this Guide with e-truth's Bible Reading Program

This nine-chapter guide was originally designed as part of e-truth's Bible-reading program. It can be used by church groups of all sizes, in a classroom setting, or by individuals. Also, go through this material at your own pace. If you prefer to go slower, work through a chapter for each meeting. Or, you may prefer to complete this material faster by working through more than one chapter per session. Use this guide in the way that works best for you and/or your group.

Features to Help You

- **Teaching Videos:** There is a teaching video for each of the nine chapters currently available through e-truth's Bible Reading Program. The videos follow closely with the content in this book. As you watch the videos, take notes and highlight valuable information. You can access the teaching videos at www.kim-christine.com.

- **Journaling Activity:** After watching the video to each chapter, do the journaling activity. If time does not allow, this activity may be completed at home between sessions.

- **meet-Me-here Journey:** This book also includes the meet-Me-here Journey, a 40-day program to help you prioritize God and develop the habits you need to draw closer to him. This program also has a journal that will help you keep track of your progress. Take this journey with a friend, a group, your church, or our online community (at www.kim-christine.com). This program is in the Bible Reading Tools section of this book.

Suggested Use for a Group Setting

1. Welcome everyone and open in prayer.

2. Watch the teaching video while following along and high-lighting valuable takeaways in this guide. Each video varies in length.

3. Do the journaling activity found in the back of each chapter after watching each video. (This may be done as a group, independently, or as homework between sessions). If a few people would like to share their journaling responses, they can do so if time permits.

4. meet-Me-here Journey/groups: During this time, break into small groups of 4-6 people. Assign a discussion leader for each group (if possible, before the session begins). The discussion leader guides the conversation by asking each person the conversation questions (found in the meet-Me-here Journey Instructions). After each person has spoken, attendees pray for one another. The meet-Me-here Journey program is located in the Bible Tools section of this book and should be read aloud (or explained) during the first meeting.

5. Close in prayer

What to Bring: Each person will need to bring this guide, something to write with, and a Bible. And, if your group is watching the videos to each chapter, you will need to have internet access.

Other Helpful Resources: You may also access other helpful resources to compliment this study, including accountability support, journal workbooks, journal PDFs, and other resources from www.kim-christine.com.

PART 1

Hearing God Through His Word

Chapter 1

GOD SPEAKS THROUGH HIS WORD

SEVERAL YEARS BACK A health scare changed the eating habits of our family. My husband's doctor warned him that he was pre-diabetic and unhealthy. From then on, I put my sergeant's cap on and started to enforce healthy eating.

One morning, as I was making coffee, my happy-go-lucky husband strolled into the kitchen and nonchalantly grabbed a box of strawberry Pop-Tarts®. So, in a whiny voice I commanded him, "Don't have Pop-Tarts for breakfast." My husband happily replied, "Okay, Honey!" Then, before I could say another word, he had poured himself a huge bowl of Fruity Pebbles cereal.

So, instead of Pop-Tarts®, he had a bowl of Fruity Pebbles cereal! Now, my exact words were, "Don't eat Pop-Tarts for break-fast." But what I meant was: "Don't eat anything unhealthy because I want us to grow old together." For that reason, I wanted him to eat something that would help him live longer. Sure, he followed my "command"—at face value. But he completely missed the heart of what I meant.

Likewise, when we read the Bible, we need to go from what the Bible says—at face value—to hear God's heart on a matter. We need to accept and believe his truths. Sadly, many people read the Bible with their hands over their ears. Their hearts are hardened by their own desires. When they read the Bible, they hear what they want to. If we are not truly seeking God, we can easily twist God's message to say whatever we want it to say.

God Wants to Speak to You. Personally. Directly. Consistently.

Because God loves you, he wants to share his heart with you. He desires to restore your hope, heal your broken heart, and guide you. He also wants to warn and correct you through his Word. You cannot live in the center of God's will without listening to him through Scripture.

But if you'll consistently take time to hear God speak to you—through his Word—your life will be transformed! You see, God's Word doesn't just give us knowledge, it gives us life.

It will help us:

- hear God's voice better
- overcome habitual sins
- destroy destructive thinking
- increase our faith

Ultimately, we will:

- experience God's presence
- walk in his power
- live out God's purpose for our lives

This guide will teach you practical step-by-step ways to hear God's voice through Scripture. By the end of this training series, you will know how to better read, understand, and apply God's Word. But first we need to know the true meaning of his message.

One Meaning, Applies Many Ways

There is only one true meaning to a biblical passage—*the meaning the biblical author intended* (as inspired by the Holy Spirit). Though a passage may apply in many ways, it still only has one meaning. Remember, the majority of the Bible is clear on what it says, especially for how to live in a close relationship with Jesus Christ. But, let's face it, some verses can be easily misunderstood. That's because the Bible was written long ago to a particular group of people addressing their specific situations.

Bridging the Culture Gap with Helpful Guidelines

Because there are huge differences between our way of life and the original biblical audience's way of life, our understanding of customs, phrases, and words greatly differ from theirs. Sometimes these differences make it hard to tell what a passage really means. That's why there are concrete guidelines (or hermeneutical principles) for reading and understanding Scripture. These guidelines help make a passage's meaning clear by bridging the gap between our cultures.

Conversations with the King

Still, reading the Bible is meant to be more than just learning about God. It's also about communicating with him in spirit and in truth. When we prayerfully read Scripture, we are personally connecting with the King of Kings, the Creator of the universe.

A Divine Message for All—And a Personal Message for You

The Bible is God's message to all of us; it reveals his will and ways for all humankind. The Bible came to us directly from God the Father through the Holy Spirit. This means the Holy Spirit inspired and worked through human authors, using their personalities and styles, to communicate exactly what God intended (2 Peter 1:20–21). It's important to realize that Scripture is "God-breathed" and that God is the ultimate author of the Bible. That's why God's message, the Bible, is infallible and always trustworthy to guide every step in our life journey.

The Bible is also a personal love letter to each one of us. That's because the Holy Spirit shows us how to personally apply God's Word to our heart, mind, actions, attitudes, and life decisions.

Remember that the Holy Spirit's work of inspiration is finished, which means that the Holy Spirit will not add new truths to the Bible or give us insights that contradict Scripture. Today, the Holy Spirit actively helps us believe, understand, and personally apply the meaning that is already there. This is the Holy Spirit's ongoing work of illumination, so you will need a reliable Bible to read from.

Bible Translations

The Old Testament (OT) was originally written in Hebrew (and very little Aramaic). The New Testament (NT) was originally written in Greek. And, to make the Bible readable, translators have taken the original languages and rewritten them in English and other languages. There are two main approaches they took to translate it: A Word-for-Word approach and a Thought-for-Thought approach.

Word-for-Word translations (or literal translation):

In this type of Bible, translators use the closest words possible from the original language to ours. Though words do not always translate exactly from one language to another, translators do their best. And, the historical and cultural aspects are left within the passages. So, to understand what the writer meant to say, readers need to bridge the cultural gap for themselves.

Advantages of Word-for-Word translations:

- This translation is better for an in-depth Bible study. You'll be able to do a word study from the original languages.

- There is less interpretation by the translator. This leaves it up to the reader to figure out the meaning of a text.

- Examples: *The English Standard Version* (ESV) and *New American Standard Bible* (NASB).

Disadvantages of Word-for-Word translations:

- This translation is harder to understand than a Thought-for-Thought translation. It takes more work and time to discern the true meaning of a passage. If you don't enjoy looking up word definitions, I'd suggest reading from a different translation.

Thought-for-Thought translations:

In this type of Bible, translators take the ideas from one language to another. There is less concern for using the closest words possible from the original language. Also, these types of translations try to make it easier to understand by removing a lot of the historical and cultural language.

Advantages of Thought-for-Thought translations:

- These translations are great for devotional use because they are easier to understand.

- These versions tend to be better for those who don't have time to look up the meaning of words.

- These translations are much easier to understand and more enjoyable for people who do not like looking up historical or cultural facts.

- Example: *New Living Translation* (NLT)

Disadvantages of Thought-for-Thought translations:

- This type of translation is not helpful for an in-depth word study of the Bible.
- This approach gives the translator a lot of "liberty" when translating. This means you're relying on another person's understanding of the text.

Here is an example of the two main approaches:

Now, let's say you send a text to a foreign exchange student that reads, "It's raining cats and dogs!" After reading this text, the foreign exchange student would be confused . . . and might think you're a little crazy. A Word-for-Word translation of the text would read, "It's raining cats and dogs." Whereas, a Thought-for-Thought translation would say, "It's raining hard."

Other translation options:

Combination: Some translations use a combination of both approaches. Examples of these types of translations include: *Holman Christian Standard Bible* (HCSB) and the *New International Version* (NIV).

Paraphrase: This type of Bible is not technically a translation because the content is not translated from the original languages. Instead, it rephrases a particular English translation. Examples of these types of versions include: *The Message* and *The Living Bible*.

When choosing a Bible translation, remember it's important to read from a reliable Bible that you understand and enjoy. It's also important to have the right attitude and approach.

The Starting Point

Before you begin reading the Bible, be sure to:

1. **Be mindful of who you are communicating with.** The Bible is more than a book that teaches us about God. The Bible is a sacred place—a sacred text—where we meet and connect with the God of the universe. With awe and reverence, be mindful that you are communicating with the King of Kings, who is worthy of all honor. At the same time, he's your loving Father who wants to share life with you. So, allow yourself to become 'undone' by surrendering your heart and mind to his loving care. Then, his Word will fulfill its purpose in your life.

2. **Ask God to speak to you through his Word.** The ultimate Bible teacher is the Holy Spirit. So, before you start reading the Bible, ask God to speak to you through it. Then, read the Bible slowly and prayerfully, paying attention to the verses that stand out to you. Once you understand the true meaning of a biblical message, patiently wait on the Holy Spirit to give you guidance for how to apply the message to your heart, mind, words, attitudes, actions, and lifestyle choices. Remember, God inspired the biblical authors to write because he *wants* to reveal himself to *you*! Expect God to help you, guide you, comfort you, correct you, and empower you through his Word.

3. **Use both your heart and mind to read the Bible.** Most of us tend to either read the Bible with our heart or mind. People who read Scripture using mainly their minds tend to believe they read it better than those who read it with their "hearts." And, those who read it with "all heart" often believe they're spiritually superior to the intellectuals. Both attitudes are prideful, and pride hinders our ability to hear from God. To be transformed by God's truth, we must read God's word with *both* our heart and mind. Plus, we need to apply the Bible's message with our entire being: heart, mind, soul, actions, and attitude.

4. **Be willing to accept what the Bible teaches.** The Bible is our ultimate authority for what we believe, what we think, what we say, and what we do. Our beliefs about God and his ways should be a direct result of what the Bible clearly teaches. We believe in the authority of the Bible because it is "God-breathed" and comes directly from God (2 Timothy 3:16; 2 Peter 1:20–21). That means we should rely on the Bible more than anyone's personal experiences, our own logic, or what any Bible teacher says. Only God's truth has the power to transform our lives, not what we think the truth is, nor what anyone else says the truth is. Believe and accept what the Bible teaches.

5. **Do your part to hear God through Scripture.** We need to know the true meaning of a biblical passage. Because God spoke to and through a specific group of people, it's important to know what he said to them first. Next, we need to look for the timeless truths within that message. Then, if we "listen", the Holy Spirit will show us how to apply those truths to our lives personally. If we do our part to understand God's Word, we can hear him speak to us through Scripture.

Chapter 1 Journaling Activity

Psalm 119 reveals the many benefits of reading and meditating on God's Word.

Read Psalm 119:1-2. According to verses 1–2, who are blessed? And, how you do you think the Word of God blesses people? How has the Word of God blessed you?

_____

_____

_____

_____

_____

Read Psalm 119:105. In this verse, God's Word reveals his direction to the psalmist. Reflecting on your lifestyle choices and habits, do you think God's Word fully directs your life decisions? In what areas of your life would you like to experience more of God's peace and direction?

_____

_____

_____

_____

_____

Read Psalm 119:97 and 119:147-148. To meditate on God's Word is to think over and dwell on scripture in and by God's presence so we can live and communicate with him. Why do you think it's important to meditate on God's Word instead of simply reading it? How will meditating on God's Word change the way you think and live?

_____

_____

_____

_____

_____

What are some consequences of not meditating on scriptures daily? Have you experienced any of these consequences in your own life?

_____

_____

_____

_____

_____

Read 2 Timothy 3:16. What does this passage tell us about the Bible? If we are to be transformed by the Bible, what heart condition or attitude do you think we need to have towards God's Word?

_____

_____

_____

_____

_____

Read 1 Thessalonians 2:13. What does this passage tell us about the Bible? And, to benefit from Scripture, what does this verse imply we should do?

_____

_____

_____

_____

_____

Chapter 2

MAKING SENSE OF GOD'S WORDS

WHEN I WAS A young woman in the mid-nineties, I had an '82 Honda Civic. I drove that little car everywhere. One day while I was driving, I noticed a puff of blue smoke coming from it, but I kept driving the car because it still got me where I needed to go. Unfortunately, the blue puffs of smoke kept getting bigger until one day, it no longer ran. When I took my car to the mechanic, he told me that I needed a new engine because I hadn't put oil in it. In those days, I did not understand how important oil was to an engine. Oops!

Likewise, it's vital to understand the true meaning of a passage. That's why we need to consider these four areas when reading Scripture:

1. Background history and cultural aspects of the Bible book (historical-cultural context)

2. Surrounding scriptures (literary context)

3. Meaning of phrases and words (the context of words and phrases)

4. Timeless message and truths within a passage

Know the historical and cultural aspects of the Bible book.

We need to know, or step inside, the historical and cultural back-story of the Bible book we are reading from. This means, when possible, finding out why the biblical author wrote to the original recipients. What circumstances were they experiencing? What attitudes, behaviors, and heart conditions needed to be confronted? Often, it's helpful to ask yourself the Five W's.

To find the historical and cultural aspects of a Bible book, you may look in 1) the Bible book's introductory section inside a study Bible 2) a Bible handbook (such as *The Essential Bible Companion*), 3) a Bible dictionary (such as the *Holman Bible Dictionary*), or 4) from Scripture itself.

Example: When reading the book of Galatians, it's helpful to know that Paul wrote to the churches in Galatia to confront false doctrines.

Understand what a passage says in light of the surrounding Scripture (e.g., Know the literary context).

To know God's message, we need to read enough Scripture at once to understand what the author intended to say. A verse does not mean anything on its own. To understand a passage, read it in light of the surrounding passages, chapters, and overall message of the Bible book. Ultimately, a passage is read in view of the testament—and even the entire Bible. This is how to read Scripture in its rightful context.

So, to understand God's heart on a matter—to understand his message in its fullness—it's necessary to read an entire section of Scripture at a time. This means reading until the topic, setting, or story changes. A section can include a chapter or so, such as in Psalms, or an entire book, such as in Philemon. And, keep in mind how the section fits in with the overall purpose and message of the Bible book.

Example: Philippians 4:13 (NKJV): "I can do all things through Christ who strengthens me." Without considering what the author meant to say, this verse seems to suggest that we can do anything we want because Christ will give us the means to. But, if we read the surrounding context, it clearly teaches that we can do (and endure) anything the Lord wills for his glory. That's because the words ". . . all things . . ." is defined by the surrounding passages.

So, God's life-giving message is not what the Bible says at face value—it's what it means and teaches. It's about the message— God's message. What did the biblical author mean when he said, "I can do all things through Christ who strengthens me"? We know what the passage means by reading the surrounding verses especially with keywords like, "so that . . .", "because . . ." etc.

Example: If I say, "I'm going to start running," you will automatically understand it to mean something specific. So, what came to your mind when I said, "I'm going to start running"? What did you assume I meant? Now, let me give you some context: "I want to be president of my college class, so I'm going to start running."

Someone could quote my exact words of, "I'm going to start running," and say that I wanted to get in shape. But you can see from the surrounding context, that's not what I meant. A lot of people quote passages from the Bible to make their point, but they don't do it in context. As a result, they completely change the meaning of God's message.

Searching for biblical answers of a particular topic: If you are looking for what the Bible teaches about a particular topic (such as healing, salvation, grace, homosexuality, etc.), remember that no single passage will cover the Bible's entire teaching of a subject. That's why it's important to look up other passages that use the same words or talk about the same subject. Then, consider what all of the scriptures teach on the topic.

You can look for answers on a topic by using the cross-reference scriptures found within the margins of many Bibles. Similar passages can also be found using a concordance (also found in the back of many Bibles). Ultimately, all scriptures must line up with the overall message of the entire Bible. The more you read the Bible, the more you will understand how all the passages fit together. Be patient; this comes with time.

Different kinds of writing styles: Read a passage according to the writing style. Because the Bible has several different types of writing in it, passages must be read differently. For example, we wouldn't read poetry like we'd read a historical account. Most importantly, take a straightforward approach to reading and interpreting the Bible. Read it literally first, and if it doesn't make sense, then interpret the figurative language appropriately. We'll discuss how to read the different genres of the Bible in chapters 6, 7, and 8.

Know the meaning of words and phrases.

To understand God's life-giving message, we also need to know what phrases and words meant to the original recipients. Most words have several possible meanings, called the semantic range. So, we'll need to find out exactly what the writer meant to say when he used a particular word or phrase.

It may be helpful to do a word study on:

- *Repeated words (keywords) that affect a verse's meaning:* Whenever you come across a word that is repeated in a passage, the biblical author is emphasizing that word for a reason.

- *Words and phrases that you don't understand:* This includes figures of speech.

- *Words and phrases that have historical and cultural significance:* As you read through a section of Scripture, pay attention to words or phrases that might have some historical or cultural background information that would be helpful to know. This may include knowing the author's thoughts towards certain people, customs, beliefs, etc. *Example:* When Jesus describes himself with the word *shepherd,* it may be helpful to look up that word in a Bible dictionary to see all their responsibilities, etc.

To do a word study:

1. Look up the word(s) in a word-study resource to see all the possible meanings the biblical writer could have meant. You may use resources such as the Blue Letter Bible app, one of the Strong's Bible concordances or *Holman's Bible Dictionary*.

2. Choose the meaning that fits best with the message of the surrounding scriptures.

3. (Optional) To do a more in-depth word study, see how the same word is used in other passages, especially by that biblical author.

   Example: When Scripture stresses the importance of "believing in Jesus for our salvation", the word "believe" affects the verse's meaning. We know that believing means more than merely believing in the existence of something. *Believing* in Jesus also means to accept and obey his teachings. We know this by 1) doing a word study of the word "believe" from the original language, 2) looking up the word in a Bible dictionary, and 3) interpreting scripture with other scripture, like in James 2:14–24.

   You do not need to do a word study on all the words in a passage. Just make sure you grasp what the writer meant to say when he used a particular phrase or word. Also, if you don't like looking up the meaning of words, simply read several different types of translations, such as the *New Living Translation* and the *English Standard Version*.

Recognize the timeless message and truths of a passage.

God is eternal—He is the same yesterday, today, and forever! (Hebrews 13:8) And, God revealed his eternal nature through the Bible using a particular group of people during a specific period of time. That's why passages that speak directly to specific situations of the original recipients can be hard to understand. Still, those passages usually include a timeless message with truths for us to follow.

Sometimes we need to look beyond the specific instructions of a passage to the heart of the command. To know if a command is still for Christians today, just ask yourself, "What does Scripture clearly and consistently teach on this topic?" When the Bible consistently says to do something, it's a timeless truth that still needs to be followed. And, if the Bible consistently and clearly teaches that something specific is a sin, avoid it because the command still applies today.

Having said that, teachings on a topic that are inconsistent or unclear might be for the original listeners only. That means they would not apply to us today. It's important that we look at the passage and ask, "What is the point of the command?" And, "How can I live out the purpose of this command?" Then, consider what all of the scriptures teach on the topic.

To determine whether a command is to be applied today or not, consider two things. The topic should be:

1. clearly and consistently taught in the New Testament

2. a part of the early churches' New Testament beliefs and routine practices. These teachings include moral truths, water baptisms, and taking communion.

For example, when Paul tells Timothy to greet someone with a holy kiss, it's a specific command for Timothy. But what's the timeless message or principle that the instruction makes known? That particular command makes it clear that we should show love to other Christians. Today if we gave someone a "holy kiss", that would be cringe-worthy. Probably not the best way to live out the reason the writer communicated it in the first place. But, one way we could show love to someone is to reach out to a hurting friend and pray with them.

All of God's instructions reveal who God is. One command or specific instruction may reveal several truths about God's nature. And vice versa, one passage about God can reveal several commands for us to follow. In the Bible, commands are the appropriate ways to respond to who God is.

Example: Proverbs 3:5–6 (NIV): "Trust in the Lord with all your heart and lean not on your own understanding; in all your ways submit to him, and he will make your paths straight."

This passage has a list of commands (the dos and don'ts) which include:

- Trust in the Lord with all your heart.
- Don't rely on your own understanding.
- Submit to him (and he'll make your paths straight).

What do these commands reveal about God's nature? Here are a few things:

- God is trustworthy.
- God sometimes does things that we can't understand.
- If you submit to God, he will direct your path.

This verse gives us a list of commands (aka things we ought to do or not do). And, those commands also reveal God's nature to us. All Scripture, in one way or another, reveals who God is and how to respond to him. It's important to read a scripture and ask yourself, "What does this scripture reveal about God?" Also ask, "How should I respond to this truth or command to live in a close relationship with him?"

The Bible Interprets Itself

Miraculously, there is unity in the overall message of the entire Bible. So, use the Bible to help interpret itself by looking up other scriptures that talk about the same topic. Because not all passages are equally clear, interpret hard-to-understand passages with clear ones to see how they fit together. Still, there are times when verses *seem* to contradict each other. In these instances, it's understood that both passages are true. And, many times, with deeper (keyword) research, these can be explained. More than that, though, we need to accept that God is much bigger than us. We will not be able to comprehend all his ways. Remember, the Bible is a supernatural book that is full of mysteries.

Example: Exodus 9:34–35 says, "When Pharaoh saw that the rain and hail, and thunder had stopped, he sinned again. He and his officials hardened their hearts. So, Pharaoh's heart was hard, and he would not let the Israelites go, just as the Lord had said through Moses." (NIV) Then, a little later, in Exodus 10:20, it says, "But the Lord hardened Pharaoh's heart, and he would not let the Israelites go." (NIV)

Exodus 9:34 says that Pharaoh hardened his own heart, then in Exodus 10:20, it says that the Lord hardened Pharaoh's heart. So, which one is correct—it seems like a paradox! When we come across scriptures that seem to contradict each other, consider *both* right.

A Supernatural Book

Most of the Bible is clear. However, we must realize, and even marvel, that the Bible is a supernatural book written by the God of the universe. As God's creation, we cannot possibly understand all the mysteries about God spoken of in the Bible. This is why there are Bible experts with different interpretations of passages today. However, with careful reading and the Holy Spirit's help, we can grasp what the Bible *intends* to reveal. And, if we seek God, he will lovingly reveal himself to us through the passages. In the next several chapters, I've combined all the aspects discussed in this chapter into step-by-step ways to know and experience God through the Bible.

Chapter 2 Journaling Activity

Read Philippians 4:13. Without considering what this verse says in light of the surrounding scriptures, what do you think this verse is saying?

_____

_____

_____

_____

_____

Read Philippians 4:8–13. How do the surrounding scriptures help shape the meaning and application of verse 13?

_____

_____

_____

_____

_____

Read Luke 10:25–37. What is the timeless message and truths revealed in the parable of the Good Samaritan?

_____

_____

_____

_____

_____

What do these truths reveal about God? What 'commands' are in these passages, and how should we respond to them?

_____

_____

_____

_____

_____

Read 1 John 4:8. What does this verse reveal about God? How should we respond to who he is? What commands would be implied by this verse?

_____

_____

_____

_____

_____

PART 2

Bible Reading Methods

Chapter 3

P-R-A-Y DEVOTIONAL BIBLE READING METHOD

WHEN MY HUSBAND AND I were first married, he worked long hours as a coffee shop manager. I felt lonely, and I desperately missed spending time with him. One night, as soon as my husband walked in the door from work, I started unmercifully complaining, "All I ever get is your leftover time!" Then, I stormed off to our bedroom like an immature teenager, plopped down on the bed, and griped to God, "All I ever get is his leftovers!" God replied, "and that's what I get from you."

Ouch! That hurt, but it was true. I was busy all the time, so I tried to fit my relationship with God inside my jam-packed schedule. My prayer life was weak, and I hardly read the Bible. Consequently, I lived my life according to my flesh, as you can tell by my story, struggled with the same sins, and ultimately lived to satisfy my own will and ways. Though I attended church regularly and served in my church, I neglected my relationship with God by only giving him my leftover time.

If we will *consistently* spend quality time in his presence, we will experience his peace and power in our lives. And, the first method I will share is a step-by-step way to read the Bible devotionally. Devotional Bible reading is prayerfully reading Scripture to connect with God. This type of Bible reading is about listening to him through scripture and communicating with him. While you are reading, the Holy Spirit may stir your heart to communicate back to God by giving him praise, expressing thanks, repenting of sins, praying the Scripture back to him, or sitting quietly in awe of who he is. When engaging Scripture this way, it's still necessary to understand passages according to what the biblical writer intended to say.

Steps for the P-R-A-Y Devotional Bible Reading Method

Step 1: Pray.

Sit quietly before God and think about his love for you. Trust the Lord with your concerns and fears, then let go of them. Ask God to speak to you through his Word. Open your heart to receive God's love, guidance, and correction through the Bible.

Step 2: Slowly read an entire section of Scripture, reflecting on the verses that stand out to you.

As you slowly and prayerfully read a section of Scripture, meditate on the verses and details that stand out to you.

Step 3: Listen to God and journal what he is speaking to you.

After reading through an entire section of Scripture, prayerfully journal each step using the P-R-A-Y Method below.

P—**Passage:** Write down the *passage(s)* that stand(s) out to you.

R—**Reveal:** Write what the passage *reveals*, especially about God and his ways.

A—**Ask:** Jot down questions to ask that will help you reflect on your life in view of the passage. (The questions should help you reflect on your heart, mind, attitudes, and life decisions in light of the passage.)

Y—Yield: Journal how God is leading you to *yield* to the passage. What is the Holy Spirit revealing to you about your heart, mind, attitudes, and/or life decisions? And, what is the Holy Spirit telling you to do specifically to apply the passage to your life?

Example of the P-R-A-Y Method: Philippians 4:6–7

P—Passage: Write down the *passage(s)* that stand(s) out to you.

Don't worry about anything; instead, pray about everything. Tell God what you need and thank him for all he has done. Then you will experience God's peace, which exceeds anything we can understand. His peace will guard your hearts and minds as you live in Christ Jesus.

R—Reveal: Write what the passage *reveals* (especially about God and his ways).

This passage reveals that I am not to worry about the circumstances I'm facing. Instead of worrying about my circumstances, I need to pray about them. I also need to trust that God will answer my prayers. I will experience God's peace when I stop worrying about what I'm going through and know that God will help me.

A—Ask: Jot down questions to ask that will help you reflect on your life in view of the passage. (The questions should help you reflect on your heart, mind, attitudes, and life decisions in light of the passage.)

Do I worry about my circumstances? What circumstances do I worry about?

Y—Yield: Journal how God is leading you to *yield* to the passage. What is the Holy Spirit revealing to you about your heart, mind, attitudes, and/or life decisions? What is the Holy Spirit telling you to do specifically to apply the passage to your life?

I worry about whether or not my children will live a life that honors God. I need to stop worrying about them and focus on God's faithfulness. I feel God saying to me, "Trust me to sanctify them, no matter what you see them doing. Do not give up praying for them. But trust Me with the results. I will draw them to Myself. Your children are in My hands.

Chapter 3 Journaling Activity

Slowly *read Psalm 86* and go through the P-R-A-Y Devotional Bible Reading Method.

P—Passage: Write the *passage* that stands out to you.

_____

_____

_____

_____

_____

R—Reveals: Write down what the passage *reveals* .

_____

_____

_____

_____

_____

A—Ask: Jot down questions to ask that will help you reflect on your life in view of the passage. (The questions should help you examine your heart, mind, actions, and attitude in light of the passage.)

_____

_____

_____

_____

_____

Y—Yield: Write down how God is leading you to *yield* to the passage.

_____

_____

_____

_____

_____

Chapter 4

THE 4-P BIBLE STUDY METHOD

I'M AN INTROVERT. I love spending time with my close group of friends, diving deep into conversation. But when I was dating my life-of-the-party husband, he was always full of "surprises".

For my 23rd birthday, my big-hearted boyfriend (now husband) told me to dress up because he was taking me to a waterfront restaurant in the Seattle area. Although I was impressed that he planned such a fancy date, I was mostly excited about spending time alone with him—just the two of us. When it came time to celebrate my birthday, we entered the high-end restaurant. Suddenly, a group of friends, mostly his, yelled, "Surprise!" My extroverted husband couldn't understand why I didn't enjoy the surprise party as much as he imagined I would. He was a little disappointed with my lack-luster response. So, to comfort him, I intentionally made the point that I wanted to spend time with him alone because I love him. Likewise, the biblical writers were inspired by the Holy Spirit to make points about God's life-giving truths.

In this chapter I share the 4-P Bible Study Method, which focuses on the point of a passage. This Bible reading approach is a simple way to study the Bible every day (especially if you don't have a lot of time). And, the 4-P method will help you focus on the meaning of a passage while engaging Scripture personally.

Steps for the 4-P Bible Study Method

P—Passage: After reading a whole section of Scripture at a time, write down the *passage* that catches your attention. A section can include a chapter or so, such as in Psalms, or an entire book, such as in Philemon.

P—Point: Write the timeless point God is making through the passage you wrote down. What is the *point* or the purpose of the passage? It may be helpful to look for words that reveal the "why" such as because, so, for, etc. (If you prefer, you may choose to write down the overall point of the section you read.)

P—Personalize: Write down how God is leading you to personally apply the passage. Ask God to show you how to *personally apply* the timeless message to your heart, mind, actions, attitude, and lifestyle choices. Take time to really meditate on the passage and listen for how God is leading you to specifically apply the passage in your own life.

P—Pray: *Pray* the Scripture back to God and journal your prayer. Ask him to help you apply the Scripture to your heart, mind, and actions. As you pray through a passage, you may choose to pray it word for word, or personalize portions of the Scripture by inserting specific names or situations into it. For example, you may choose to put your name in place of pronouns or nouns used in a particular passage. Simply allow the Scripture to shape your prayers.

Example of the 4-P Method: Read 1 Corinthians 13

P—Passage: Write down the *passage(s)* that stand(s) out to you.

13:4–7 (NLT): "Love is patient and kind. Love is not jealous or boastful or proud or rude. It does not demand its own way. It is not irritable, and it keeps no record of being wronged. It does not rejoice about injustice but rejoices whenever the truth wins out. Love never gives up, never loses faith, is always hopeful, and endures through every circumstance."

P—Point: Write down the *point* of the passage.

This passage is pointing out that I need to be willing to be selfless and give up my own desires for the good of other people.

P—Personalize: Write how God is leading you to *personally apply* the passage.

I need to stop being selfish with my schedule. I also need to be more flexible when it comes to my children's routines and schedules.

P—Pray: *Pray* the scriptures back to God and journal your prayer.

God, please forgive my selfishness. Jesus help me be patient with my children and their schedules. Help me to not be irritable when my schedule is not followed.

Chapter 4 Journaling Activity

Read Philippians 1 and go through the 4-P Bible study method.

P—Passage: Write the *passage* that stands out to you.

_____

_____

_____

_____

_____

P—Point: Write down the timeless *point* of the passage.

_____

_____

_____

_____

P—Personalize: Write how to *personally apply* the passage.

_____

_____

_____

_____

_____

P—Pray: *Pray* the scriptures back to God and journal the prayer.

_____

_____

_____

_____

_____

Chapter 5

THE K-I-N-G-S-! BIBLE STUDY METHOD

From the time I was a young girl I had always dreamed of my big day—my wedding day. I wanted the fairy tale wedding. Once I became engaged I started planning an elegant ceremony. I decided to walk down a candlelit aisle to a classy song performed live by a saxophone player.

It just so happened that a friend of mine personally knew an experienced saxophonist. Well, I assumed he was experienced—at least that's what I had heard. When my big day came, everything was story-book perfect. Then, it was time for me to grace the aisle to the lovely saxophone music. But to my horror, the musician painfully screeched out an unrecognizable tune. There I was, with no choice but to walk down the elegantly decorated aisle to the loud, squealing horn.

Thankfully, I can laugh about this mishap. As funny as it was, though, there is a lesson we can learn: Don't assume to know something without getting the facts straight.

Likewise, without truly reflecting on the meaning of God's Word, it's easy to assume that we understand the meaning of a passage at first glance. Or, we can rely too much on what a trusted Bible teacher or preacher says. But assuming we know what God's Word says may cause us to miss out on his life-changing truth.

That's why we need to know how to read and understand Scripture for ourselves.

Based on the concrete guidelines for understanding Scripture (aka hermeneutical guidelines), I've created the K-I-N-G-S-! Bible Study Method. The K-I-N-G-S-! Method includes six steps. Once you complete the first two steps (K-I), complete steps 4-6 (N-!) for each paragraph (or a smaller portion of scripture) within the section you are studying. Also, if you desire a more academic type of study, follow the Academic Option offered in steps 1–3.

Once you've selected the passage you will study, ask God to speak to you through His Word. Then, slowly and prayerfully follow these steps:

Step 1: "K"—Know the story behind the Bible book you're reading from (e.g., the historical-cultural context).

The Bible is made up of 66 small books. Each book was written for a reason. Each one has a backstory. Before you begin reading, you'll want to know why the biblical author wrote the book in the first place (its purpose) and about the people he was writing to (the audience). As you read the backstory, ask yourself: who, what, when, where, and why. (Example questions: Who was the book written to? Why was it written? What were they experiencing/ feeling?)

To find the Bible book's purpose (the story behind the Bible book you're reading from) you may look in a Bible handbook, a background commentary, in the Scripture itself, or your personal Bible may have it in the Bible book's introduction. If you prefer looking for the backstory directly from Scripture, often the biblical author shares why he wrote it towards the beginning or ending of the book. Sometimes the author doesn't share the "why," but you can discern the book's purpose by reading through it to see what the author is mainly addressing.

Helpful Tip: Reading the backstory often feels "dry," but if you'll imagine what the original audience was going through, putting yourself in their shoes, the Scripture will really come to life.

Academic Option: Having a general understanding for why the book was written will work great, but feel free to read from several resources and gather as much background information (i.e., the historical-cultural context) as you'd like.

What to Journal: Write down what you learned about why the book was written. Also, jot down anything else you found interesting about the background.

Step 2: "I"—Identify the overall message— a section of Scripture at a time (e.g., the literary context).

Read through the entire section of Scripture your passage is found in to get a feel for the big picture, the overall message. Then, ask yourself what one word or phrase sums up the overall message.

Remember, to understand God's message in its fullness, it's necessary to read an entire section at a time. This means reading until the topic, setting, or story changes. A section can include a chapter or so, such as in Psalms, or an entire book, such as in Philemon. As you read keep in mind what the passage and Bible book says as a whole. This is how to read scripture in its rightful context.

Helpful Tip: If you're struggling to find the overall meaning, it may be helpful to pay attention to repeated words. Repeated words often reveal what the biblical writer is emphasizing. Then, look at the repeated word(s) and ask yourself, "What is the writer mostly saying about these words?"

Academic Option: Read through an entire book, in one sitting if possible, and create an outline based on the overall message/ points. It is up to you how detailed your outline is (unless a professor instructs you otherwise).

What to Journal: After reading the section your passage is found in, jot down one word, phrase, or sentence that sums up the overall message of the section.

Step 3: "N"—Notice what a passage says and the details that stand out to you—one paragraph or so at a time.

After completing step 2, zoom in and slowly read the section again, focusing on one paragraph (or smaller portion of scripture) at a time. Notice what each paragraph (or smaller portion of scripture) reveals—especially about God and his ways. Take time to really hear what the life-giving passage tells, shows, or expresses.

Then, notice the details that stand out to you in the paragraph (or smaller portion of scripture). Details shed light on the meaning of the passage. Details you may notice include: keywords, repeated words, examples to follow or avoid, warnings, commands to obey, comparing and contrasting, figures of speech, lists of characteristics, conditional words (if, when, after, etc.), words that show the purpose (in order that, so, so that, because, for, therefore, etc.), action words (verbs of all forms) and anything else that stands out to you.

Helpful Tips

- When you come across seemingly meaningless or obscure verses and details, ask yourself how they relate to the overall message.

- As words grab your attention, or to clarify what a passage says, you may want to look them up in a word-study resource. You may also find it helpful to read and compare a variety of modern Bible translations, such as a *Holman Christian Standard Bible* (HCSB), *New International Version* (NIV), and *New Living Translation* (NLT).

Academic Option: Take time to look up keywords, unfamiliar phrases and words, and cultural aspects in a Bible dictionary or word-study resource. Analyze sentence structure and diagram sentences, using the same subjects, verbs, and objects in the text. Remember, all sentences must be understood in view of the surrounding passages.

What to Journal: As you read through the section, jot down the main points within each paragraph of the section you are reading from. Then, write down the details that stand out to you. Also, write down repeated words and unfamiliar words along with their definitions.

Step 4: "G"—Grasp the message given to the original recipients.

Grasp the message given specifically to the original recipients by looking at what you discovered from steps 1–3. Ask yourself: "What did the biblical author want *them* to do and believe specifically? How did he want *them* to respond to the message?"

Remember: The biblical authors were moved by the Holy Spirit to write to a certain group of people to teach, correct, warn, guide, and give them instructions for how to live in a right relationship with God. That's why we need to first understand what the message meant to the original recipients.

What to Journal: Jot down what the author wanted his biblical audience to do, believe, and understand specifically. It's best to write this as past tense.

Step 5: "S"—Seek the timeless message and truths.

Looking at the message given to the original recipients (step 4), seek the timeless message and truths from the passage. Timeless passages and commands include truths about who God is and truths for how to live according to his ways. There may be several timeless truths revealed in one passage, or even one command.

Usually, God's timeless message and truths are plainly written in Scripture. You can recognize them because they 1) describe God's nature and ways, 2) can be applied by anyone, anywhere, at any time, and 3) are clearly and consistently taught throughout Scripture. Examples include: God is holy, do not worry, pray at all times, etc.

Other times, you will need to look beyond the specific aspect(s) of a passage to the heart of the message. When you read a passage that is specific to the original recipients, ask yourself, "Why was this command given to them?" and "How can I live out the purpose of this passage?" The purpose for the command reveals the timeless message and truths that we need to live by. Keywords may reveal why a specific command was given (so, for, therefore, because, in order that, etc.).

Example: Ephesians 5:18 (ESV): "And do not get drunk with wine . . ." The purpose of this command is so that Christians won't be hindered in their walk with God because it breaks their fellowship with him. So, to live out the purpose of this command, Christians would not want to get drunk or high using any substance (not just wine).

Also, to find the timeless truth in a Bible story, look to see what the story shows us about God and his ways by how he interacts with people. This will usually be the moral of the story. So, when reading a Bible story, ask yourself: "What does the story teach us about God and his ways?" Stories often illustrate truths that are clearly taught elsewhere in Scripture.

What to Journal: Write down God's timeless truths that declare who he is and what his ways are.

Step 6: "!"—Apply God's word to your life.

Reflecting on the timeless message, ask God to show you how to apply the truths to your daily life, practically and specifically. Patiently wait for God to show you how to apply the passage to your heart, mind, actions, attitude, words, and choices.

Scripture can be applied in many ways. Questions to help guide you in responding to God's Word include: "Does the attitude of my heart line up with God's Word? Is there a life-giving truth to be meditated on and believed? Does my lifestyle align with God's will and ways? Is there a command or an instruction to obey? Is there a sin to repent from? A warning to be aware of?

Is there a promise to hold on to? What Bible passage do I need to pray through?"

What to Journal: Write down what God is speaking to you and ways he wants you to apply the timeless message specifically to your life.

Example of the K-I-N-G-S-! Method: Colossians 2:6–7 (NLT):

Step 1: "K"—Know the story behind the Bible book you're reading from.

While in prison, Paul wrote to the church in Colossae to combat the false teachings. He warned them not to believe the false teachers, but to remember that they were saved in Christ alone.

Step 2: "I"—Identify the overall message—a section of Scripture at a time.

Overall, this section tells us that we are spiritually complete in Christ alone.

Step 3: "N"—Notice what a passage says and the details that stand out to you—one paragraph at a time.

- Continue: We must continue in our pursuit of Christ. It is not a one-time decision, but a lifestyle.

- Keyword: "Rooted" in Christ. It's a steadfast commitment, not based on feeling, but on faith.

Step 4: "G"—Grasp the message given to the original recipients.

Paul told the Colossians to continue to grow in the Lord. And Paul warned them to believe in the truth they were taught.

Step 5: "S"—Seek the timeless message and truths.

- A Christian's relationship with Jesus should develop and mature.
- Christians must continually choose to live for God.
- We must believe what the Bible teaches, not trust teachers who teach doctrines that differ from the teachings found in Scripture.

Step 6: "!"—Apply God's word to your life.

I must choose to put Christ first despite my jam-packed schedule. This means I'll need to wake up 40 minutes earlier than I already do to spend time with God. Right now, my heart is complacent. I will need to be intentional about growing in Christ.

Chapter 5 Journaling Activity

Read Colossians 2:6–10 and prayerfully go through these steps:

K—Know the story behind the Bible book you're reading from (historical-cultural context):

The Bible book's background may include the who, what, when, where, and why of the book. The Bible book's purpose (the story behind the Bible book) can be found in the Scripture itself, a Bible handbook, background commentary, or your personal Bible may have it in the Bible book's introduction.

Write out the purpose for the book (the book's background information).

_____

_____

_____

_____

_____

I—Identify the overall message—a section of Scripture at a time (literary context):

Read through the section of Scripture your passage is found in to get a feel for the big picture, or the overall message. Then, ask yourself what one word or phrase sums up the overall message. A section can include a chapter or so, such as in Psalms, or an entire book, such as in Philemon. Read the passage in light of the Bible book's purpose.

Jot down one word, phrase, or sentence that sums up the overall message of the section.

_____

_____

_____

_____

_____

N—Notice what a passage says and the details that stand out to you—one paragraph at a time:

Information you may want to notice include: Repeated words (keywords); commands; warnings/consequences; promises; conditional clauses; purpose statements (in order that, so that, etc.); verbs; figurative language/descriptive language; dialogue/conversations; examples (both negative and positive); truths; explanations.

Jot down the main point for each paragraph (or smaller portion of scripture) within the section you are studying. Then, write down the details that stand out to you. You may want to write down unfamiliar words along with their definitions.

_____

_____

_____

_____

_____

G—Grasp the message given to the original recipients:

After looking over steps 1–3, summarize the biblical author's message to the *original* recipients; what specifically did the author want them to do, believe, or understand?

Write out a past-tense statement that summarizes what the author wanted the original recipients to do, believe, or understand specifically.

_____

_____

_____

_____

_____

S—Seek the timeless truths:

A passage or command is timeless if it: 1) reveals God's character or how to live according to his ways or 2) includes moral truths and/or specific commands that are consistently taught and supported throughout Scripture, specially in the New Testament and 3) can be applied today by anyone from anywhere. (A passage may also reveal something about human nature, the church, etc.)

Write down the timeless message and truths revealed in the passage.

_____

_____

_____

_____

_____

!—Apply God's word to your life:

Reflecting on the timeless message and truths, ask God to show you how to personally apply the truths to your life. Be still and wait for the Holy Spirit to reveal how he wants you to respond to his Word.

Journal how God is leading you to apply the passage to your heart, mind, actions, attitude, and life decisions.

_____

_____

_____

_____

_____

PART 3

Tips for Reading the Different Genres in the Bible

Chapter 6

TIPS FOR READING BIBLICAL POETRY

WHEN MY TEENAGE SON was learning how to drive a car I warned him not to text and drive. I repeatedly told him that he could get seriously hurt or worse. So, my son knew that he shouldn't text and drive. But just because he knew the rules didn't mean he fully realized the consequences of disobeying them.

I've also said, "Imagine you're driving your car and quickly check your friend's text message. When you look up, you're just about to hit a semi-truck—head on! All your plans of going to college and living on your own are gone in a moment. Imagine the grief your dad and I would have to endure for the rest of our lives!"

In the past, I've always been straightforward with my son about the dangers of texting while driving. But, by using these emotional words, I tried to get him to see the importance of obeying me. I wasn't teaching him something new. Instead, I was trying to get him to think about the consequences of not obeying my instructions.

In the same way, God uses poetry to stir our hearts so we will respond to his message. Poetry doesn't teach us new biblical truths but encourages us to respond to what he's already taught us elsewhere in Scripture.

How God Uses Poetry

The Old Testament is filled with God-inspired poetry, including most of the wisdom books, prophetic books, and all of the Psalms. God uses poetry to help us recognize the lifestyle of a righteous person (Psalm 1), reflect on his faithfulness (Psalm 98) and warn us of the consequences of ignoring his Word (Psalm 1).

Other poetry, especially the Psalms, helps us worship God. We can use them as an example to better express our hearts and feelings for him. Poetry uses emotional words and pictures to get us to slow down and reflect on who God is.

The Art and Science of Poetry

There are many ways of writing, but the two main kinds are prose (our normal way of writing) and poetry. In prose, thoughts are organized into paragraphs. In poetry, a "paragraph" is called a stanza. And, stanzas usually have four lines (called verses).

The lines in a stanza can work together to emotionally express a truth or feeling through a form known as parallelism. Most often, the first line will express a strong feeling or truth. Then, the second line will usually re-emphasize the same feeling or truth of the first line by 1) using different words 2) furthering the thought more, or 3) stating the truth in a contrasting way.

That means in a 4-line stanza, there's usually one main truth or feeling being expressed for every two lines. Sometimes, though, all the lines in a stanza will stress the same truth or feeling.

Let's look at some examples of how lines work together to emphasize a biblical truth:

Psalm 1:6 (NKJV) : "For the Lord knows the way of the righteous, but the way of the ungodly shall perish." Often, the second line emphasizes the same truth of the first line in a contrasting way.

Psalm 46:7 (ESV) : "The Lord of hosts is with us; the God of Jacob is our fortress." Other times, the lines work together to express the same truth about God using different words or images in the second line.

Psalm 104:5 (ESV) : "He set the earth on its foundations, so that it should never be moved." Sometimes, the first line introduces a thought or truth. Then, the second line develops it by giving a reason. Other times, the first line will ask a question, and the second line gives the answer.

Poets Expressed God's Truths in Creative Ways

The biblical poets were inspired by the Holy Spirit to express God's truth creatively. Here are a few helpful tips for how to read them.

Biblical poets would often use hyperboles, or purposeful exaggerations, to make their point.

Example: Psalm 42:3 (NKJV): "My tears have been my food day and night . . ." Here, the psalmist purposefully exaggerates his sorrow to express his unbearable grief.

When you come across a purposeful exaggeration, or a hyperbole, just focus on the point the poet is trying to make. What's he trying to say? Today, someone may exaggerate and say, "If I can't get a Smartphone, I'll die." Obviously, that person wouldn't really keel over if they didn't get a Smartphone. No, they're making the point that they really (really, really) want one. In the same way, if we focus on what the verses say literally, we'll completely miss the point being made.

The biblical poet would ask a rhetorical question to make a point.

These questions are meant to be reflected on, not answered. When reading a rhetorical question, reflect on the point being made by the question.

Example: In Job 38:4 (ESV), God asks Job, "Where were you when I laid the foundation of the earth?" God was not expecting an answer; God already knew the answer. Instead, God wanted Job to reflect on the fact that he is the Creator, and Job did not have the right to question him.

The biblical poet often uses a particular image to describe a feeling or truth.

The majority of these images are called similes or metaphors. As you come across images, reflect on what the image communicates. Most of the time, the biblical writer is comparing a specific characteristic of an image to a feeling or a truth. Remember, there is a logical reason the biblical poet used a particular image to describe something, often about God.

Usually, you'll be able to tell what the image represents by simply reading the surrounding passages. But, if you don't know what an image means or why it's being compared to something, you may want to look up the image or word in 1) a Bible dictionary or 2) the original Hebrew or Greek word using a concordance or other word-study resource.

Example: Psalm 1:3 (ESV): "(He) is like a tree planted by streams of water that yields its fruit in its season." Here the psalmist is comparing a righteous man with a tree that is flourishing and producing fruit. You know it's a comparison because the writer uses the words, "He is *like* . . ."

Sometimes comparisons aren't as obvious because the words "like" or "as" aren't used. Here is an example of a metaphor: "The Lord is my . . . shield" Psalm 28:7 (NIV). In this verse, the Lord is being compared to a physical shield. A shield protects and guards. Of course, the Lord is not a physical shield, but the verse emphasizes that God is our ultimate protector.

The biblical poet will often say the opposite of what is literally meant (irony).

Example: Job 12:2 (NKJV): Job sarcastically says to his friends, "No doubt . . . wisdom will die with you." Job did not really mean what he said. Reading the surrounding passages makes it clear that Job considered his friend's "wisdom" to be foolish. Job actually meant the opposite of what he said.

To know if a writer meant the opposite of what he said, pay attention to what the surrounding passages reveal.

The biblical poets would often use one word in their writing that stands for another word (figures of substitution).

Example: Joel 2:28 (NKJV) ". . . I will pour out my Spirit on all flesh." The word "flesh" substitutes the word "people". When you come across phrases or words that don't make sense, it's possible that the word stands for something else altogether.

Biblical poets often used sayings, called idioms, that were not meant to be taken literally.

Example: Matthew 8:21 (ESV): "Another of his disciples said to him, 'Lord, let me first go and bury my father.'" To "bury my father" was an expression that meant, "collect my inheritance". The person who said this probably believed that he couldn't afford to follow Jesus until his father, who was alive and well, died and he inherited enough money.

There are a lot of sayings throughout the Bible, including poetry. God used writers from a different culture and time to write the Bible. Many of the sayings in Scripture were only used by that particular group of people. That means we'll need to learn these sayings as we come across them in our reading.

Think about the American saying, "stabbed in the back". People who aren't familiar with that expression can't figure it out using a dictionary or word-study resource. The most accurate way to determine what these sayings mean is to hear and understand them in their own culture.

If you come across something that sounds "odd" in Scripture, it may be an idiom. So, look up the verse in a biblical resource to see what the saying means. An expositor Bible commentary would be helpful, or simply read the passage from a different Bible translation (such as *The Message* or *The Living Bible*).

How to Hear God through Poetry

Remember that poetry is meant to be read differently than our standard type of writing. Poetry is meant to be felt and experienced, not dissected analytically. That's why I recommend using either the *P-R-A-Y Devotional Bible Reading Method* or the *4-P Bible Study Method* when reading poetry. Most importantly, use your imagination and follow the flow of emotions and images from one line to the next. Then, reflect on the truth or feeling being expressed.

When you come across descriptive words and images (figures of speech), picture them in your mind. Then, reflect on the truth or feeling the image conveys. The more lifelike the picture is in your mind, the more meaningful your experience will be.

Remember, there is a logical reason the writer used a particular image. You'll know the reason by looking at the context of the poem—at the verses that surround the image. What truth or feeling is being emphasized with the image? Usually, the poet intended to compare one aspect of an image with a truth, usually about God, or a feeling.

Example: "The Lord is my . . . shield." Here, the Lord is being compared to a physical shield to emphasizes the point that God is the ultimate protector.

If you do not understand why a particular image was used, look to find what the image represents or means. To do this, read from another Bible translation. Or, look up the word in a Bible dictionary or a word-study resource.

When you read poetry, focus on the truth being expressed—the meaning intended by the author. Remember that God's truths are clearly taught and supported throughout the Bible.

Chapter 6 Journaling Activity

Slowly *read Psalm 1* and follow the P-R-A-Y Method.

P—Passage: Write down the *passage* that stands out to you.

_____

_____

_____

_____

_____

R—Reveals: Write what the passage *reveals.*

_____

_____

_____

_____

_____

A—Ask: Jot down questions to ask that will help you reflect on your life in view of the passage.

_____

_____

_____

_____

_____

Y—Yield: Write down how God is leading you to *yield* to the passage.

_____

_____

_____

_____

_____

Chapter 7

TIPS FOR READING THE OLD TESTAMENT

WHEN I WAS A young girl, my pastor shared a true story to show God's love:

> There was a young woman who didn't know God. One day at work, she overheard her co-workers talking to each other. One worker said, "If you're ever in trouble, if you're ever in danger, just call on the name of Jesus. He will save you." The next day, the woman, who didn't know God, was attacked by a man in her car. Remembering what her co-workers said, she cried out, "Jesus!" Miraculously, her car horn started going off and her lights began blinking. It scared the man, and he ran away.

This story changed my view of God. I no longer saw God as distant and uninvolved. The story allowed me to taste God's goodness as I reflected on how God intervened on behalf of a helpless woman. Because of this story, I still call out "Jesus!" whenever I feel like I'm in trouble. God speaks to us through stories in the Old Testament, too.

The Old Testament reveals who God is as the creator, who we are as his creation, and includes stories of how God miraculously moved in the lives of people throughout history. It also shows us that we are sinners who need a savior and points us to the life and work of his coming son, Jesus.

When reading and interpreting the Old Testament, keep in mind that God continued to reveal himself and his plan for salvation over time. So, consider how a passage fits within God's progressive revelation. Although God is the same yesterday, today, and forever, the promises and laws that he gave to Abraham and his descendants in the Old Testament may not necessarily be for us today.

In the Old Testament, there are four main kinds, or genres, of writing: Stories (called Historical Narratives), Law, Wisdom, and Prophecy.

Here are some helpful tips for reading the four main genres found in the Old Testament.

Reading His Stories (Historical Narratives)

Almost every book in the Bible contains stories about who God is. Bible books filled with stories include Genesis, Exodus, Numbers, Joshua, Judges, 1 and 2 Samuel, 1 and 2 Kings, 1 and 2 Chronicles, Ezra and Nehemiah. These stories reveal how God miraculously moved in the lives of people throughout history.

His stories, called historical narratives, are to reveal God's nature through people and past events. Stories show us who God is and reveal his glory. Also, the stories show us that we need God and point to Christ.

To find the timeless message in a Bible story, see what the story reveals about God and his ways. What does the story show us about God? When reading a biblical story, ask yourself, "What is the moral of the story?" Stories point to truths that are clearly taught elsewhere in Scripture.

When reading Bible stories:

Look for God's Divine Intervention: Look for how God intervened in the lives of people throughout history. These stories show us who God is by how he interacted with people.

Listen to What the Narrator Says: Also, "listen to" the narrator, the person who is telling the story. Remember, the narrator is speaking on God's behalf and gives divine insight into the heart and point of the story.

Look at the Introduction and Conclusion of a Bible Book: Sometimes the biblical author tells what the main message is towards the beginning or ending of a Bible book.

Pay Attention to Dialogue: Remember, the author shared that particular dialogue for a reason. Those words reveal the heart condition of the person who was talking, whether they loved and followed God or had evil intentions.

Repeated Words, Phrases, and Ideas: Pay attention for repeated words, because they show us what the writer was emphasizing. For example, in Job the phrase "he was a righteous man" was used several times. The suffering that Job endured had nothing to do with his sin. Instead, the book of Job shows us God's glory through Job's suffering. Though Job wasn't sinless (no one is), the writer made a point that God considered Job to be righteous.

Reading and Interpreting the Law

The 613 laws God gave to Moses and his people on Mount Sinai were to express God's will for Israel. These laws are found in the books of Leviticus and Deuteronomy.

These laws helped govern every aspect of their lives, including their worship and ceremonial practices, daily conduct, and moral character. Today, we only follow the moral laws (laws relating to God's will, ways, and nature) that have been re-affirmed in the New Testament.

When reading the laws, look for the principle, or purpose, of the law. Ask yourself, "Why was this law given? How did this law help people live morally?" For example, the law in Deuteronomy 7:3 commands, "You shall not marry them (the Gentiles) . . ." This law was given so that God's people would not be led astray. Today, the purpose of the law remains: We should not marry those who would lead us away from God. God reaffirms this "law" in 2 Corinthians 6:14.

Sometimes it's hard to tell what the purpose of a law is. That's because some laws were primarily given to keep Israel separate from their idol-worshipping neighbors. At times, it may be helpful to have knowledge of the Hebrew lifestyle and of the covenants. These laws were specifically for Israel under the Old Covenant. Today, we are under the New Covenant, which is for all people. That's why we only follow the moral laws that are re-affirmed in the New Testament.

Reading Wisdom Books

The Bible teaches that the beginning of wisdom is fear (Proverbs 9:10), or to put it simply, wisdom is making choices out of reverence for God. This means a wise person will seek God's will, follow God's guidance, live according to his ways, and make decisions that honor and please him—in every area of life. Wisdom books include Job, Ecclesiastes, Lamentations, and Proverbs.

Proverbs: Proverbs shares practical ways to live according to God's will. Understand the proverb in light of the chapter. Then, look for the timeless messages and determine how to apply them appropriately today.

Lamentations and Job: These books are written in lengthy conversations. When reading these books, read and understand an entire book as a whole. For example, when reading Job, it's important to understand that chapters 3—37 are foolish advice given by Job's well-meaning friends—and not for us to follow. If you don't read an entire book in one sitting, just make sure you know how each section fits into the book as a whole (e.g., know the context of each verse).

Ecclesiastes: Ecclesiastes was written as a monologue. In other words, the author, Solomon, is basically having a conversation with himself. At times he sounds like he's contradicting himself, but that's because he's working out the answer "aloud" in his writing. He comes up with the solution in chapter 12: Life is short, and only God can bring life meaning and purpose. So, make sure to understand each verse in light of the entire book.

Reading the Prophetic Books

The prophetic books include the Old Testament books of Isaiah through Malachi. Although God raised up prophets to predict future events, the majority of the prophecies were for events in the near future of that time and have already been fulfilled.

For the most part, God used prophets to speak on his behalf, calling his people back to a covenant relationship with himself. Most prophetic books can basically be summed up as God crying out to his people, "I love you! Come back to me!"

Though Israel had times where they were faithful to God, most of the time they weren't. They usually sinned against God by taking advantage of the poor and participating in idolatry. The prophets usually: 1) confronted God's people for their sin, 2) called them to repent, 3) warned of the coming judgment if they didn't repent, and 4) proclaimed that they would be restored in God's timing after repentance.

Also, as you read the prophetic books, you'll notice there's a lot of judgment-type prophecies. When reading these types of passages, it's important to hear God's plea for his people to repent. These prophecies sound like they contradict each other. But it was understood that if the people would've truly repented, God would have forgiven and restored them without judgment. (Sadly, God's children, the Israelites, did not turn from their evil, rebellious ways and faced God's judgment.)

Usually, God called prophets to confront specific groups of people about their sins or their situations. But, without realizing it, sometimes the prophets also spoke beyond their own knowledge about future events. Though the prophet had one meaning in mind, the scripture is applied differently later in the New Testament.

Because most of the prophecies have been fulfilled, we now understand how they point to Jesus's first coming. And, the New Testament writers were inspired by the Holy Spirit to use many

Old Testament prophecies to prove that Jesus is the ultimate fulfillment of them. Still, we need to know what the message meant to the original audience and why God spoke to them. What heart conditions and situations did the prophet confront? What did God want to correct? Were the people doing something that displeased God? This is what the prophets answered.

Reading Apocalyptic Literature

Apocalyptic literature is a specific type of prophecy that mostly predicts disaster using lots of seemingly weird symbols and imagery. These scriptures, like other prophetic books, are very hard to interpret—even for Bible experts. We find this type of writing in parts of Daniel, Ezekiel, Zechariah, and a lot in Revelation. These passages are often misinterpreted because people are quick to assign current events to specific prophecies. Some things will not be made clear to us except in the fullness of time.

Hearing God through the Old Testament

The Old Testament is filled with stories, wisdom, and prophecies that show God's love, greatness, wonder, judgment, and majesty. Just look for God's activity throughout the stories and Bible books. Use your imagination to step inside the passages to experience the stories. Also, notice the similarities and differences between the people in the text and yourself. What can you relate to? Then, focus on what pleases and displeases God. Then, ask yourself, "How can I become closer to God?" Expect God to show himself to you as you read the Old Testament.

Chapter 7 Journaling Activity

Read the book of Obadiah (focusing on 1:11–12) and go through the steps below:

K—Know the story behind the Bible book you're reading from (historical-cultural context):

The Bible book's background may include the who, what, when, where and/or why of the book. The Bible book's purpose can be found in the scriptures themselves, a Bible handbook, background commentary, or your personal Bible may have it in the Bible book's introduction.

Write out the purpose for the book.

_____

_____

_____

_____

_____

I—Identify the overall message—a section of Scripture at a time (literary context):

Read through the section of Scripture your passage is found in to get a feel for the big picture, the overall message. Then, ask yourself what one word or phrase sums up the overall message. A section can include a chapter or so, such as in Psalms, or an entire book, such as in Philemon. Read the passage in light of the Bible book's purpose.

Jot down one word, phrase, or sentence that sums up the overall message of the section.

_____

_____

_____

_____

_____

N—Notice what a passage says and the details that stand out to you—one paragraph at a time:

Information you may want to notice includes: Repeated words (keywords); verbs; commands; warnings/consequences; promises; conditional clauses; purpose statements (in order that, so that, etc.); figurative language/descriptive language; dialogue/conversations; examples (both negative and positive); truths; explanations.

Jot down the main point for each paragraph (or smaller portion of scripture) within the section you are studying. Then, write down the details that stand out to you. You may want to write down unfamiliar words along with their definitions.

_____

_____

_____

_____

_____

G—Grasp the message given to the original recipients:

After looking over steps 1–3, summarize the biblical author's message to the *original* recipients; what specifically did the author want them to do, believe, or understand?

Write out a past-tense statement that summarizes what the author wanted the original recipients to do, believe, or understand specifically.

_____

_____

_____

_____

_____

S—Seek the timeless truths:

A passage or command is timeless if it: 1) reveals God's character or how to live according to his ways or 2) includes moral truths and/or specific commands that are consistently taught and supported throughout Scripture, especially in the New Testament and 3) can be applied today by anyone from anywhere. (A passage may also reveal something about human nature, the church, etc.)

Write down the timeless message and truths revealed in the passage.

_____

_____

_____

_____

_____

!—Apply God's word to your life:

Reflecting on the timeless message and truths, ask God to show you how to personally apply the truths to your life. Be still and wait for God to reveal how he wants you to respond to his Word.

Journal how God is leading you to apply the passage to your heart, mind, actions, attitude, and life decisions.

_____

_____

_____

_____

_____

Chapter 8

TIPS FOR READING THE NEW TESTAMENT

IN 2001, MY HUBBY and I decided to move from the greater Seattle area to a small town in North Dakota to attend a bible college. It felt like we stepped off of planet Earth. Seriously, though, I love that town and the bible college we attended.

Every weekday morning, they held a chapel service. One day, a lady obnoxiously interrupted the sermon and shouted, "Um . . . excuse me, I can't hear you!" I was taken back by her lack of concern for social norms. But, I have to admit, when I hear a sermon that does not line up with Scripture, I want to confront the false teaching in the same way. I'd like to interrupt and say, "Um . . . excuse me, that's not in the Bible!"

Paul, who authored most of the New Testament, wrote many letters to confront and correct false teachings. Most of all, the New Testament bears witness to the life and work of Jesus Christ, God's son and the Savior of the world. It also reveals how to live in a close relationship with God, through Jesus Christ, by walking in the power of the Holy Spirit.

Keep in mind that the New Testament is a continuing revelation of God's will and ways. So, pay attention to how the life-saving work of Jesus Christ changes some Old Testament practices, promises, and precepts. And, as you are reading the New Testament, if a word, phrase, or concept doesn't make sense, it may be helpful to see what the Old Testament says about it. The biblical writers assumed their audience knew the Old Testament. In fact, the Old Testament is the foundation of the New Testament and builds upon it.

There are four main types of writing in the New Testament: Gospels, Parables, Church History (Acts) and Epistles (e.g., the letters).

Here are some helpful tips for reading the different types of writing found in the New Testament.

Reading the Gospels

The Gospels are stories, or historical accounts, of Jesus's life that testify to who he was—and is—the Savior of the World, Messiah, and King! The Gospels include Matthew, Mark, Luke, and John.

Matthew, Mark, and Luke are called the Synoptic Gospels because they include many of the same stories. When writing, the authors didn't change the facts about Jesus's stories. Instead, they highlighted different aspects of those stories to meet the specific needs of their intended audience. For example, Matthew wrote to the Jewish people and wanted them to know that Jesus was the Messiah they had been waiting for. On the other hand, Luke writes to the needs of Gentile Christians.

When reading the Gospels, focus on one story at a time. Also, because the writers were led by the Holy Spirit to put the stories in a particular order, you may find it helpful to read the surrounding stories to look for connections between them. What are the similarities and differences between the stories? Sometimes there will be a shared biblical truth between them. Ask yourself, "How does the point of this story fit in with the surrounding narratives (or stories)?"

Reading Parables

Parables are stories that Jesus used to teach biblical truths. As Matthew 13:10–12 reveals, he used them to: 1) hide the truth from those who will not believe and 2) to reveal the truth to those who do believe. Jesus used (and still uses) parables to motivate listeners to respond to his life-giving truth.

When reading parables, look for the life lesson of each main character or main group of people (e.g., the Pharisees, the crowd, etc.). Most parables will only make one or two main points. Also, don't focus too much on the details because they are just there to make the story more life-like. Sometimes, Jesus explains the meanings of his parables after he tells the story.

Example: In Matthew 13:3–9, Jesus gave the parable of the sower and then gave an explanation for the parable in 13:18–23.

Also, pay attention to cultural words and aspects. Jesus first told the parables to people whose lifestyles are very different from our own. That's why looking up cultural words in a Bible dictionary will give us more insight into the parables' meaning.

Example: Luke 10:25–37: In the parable of the Good Samaritan, the Samaritan was considered an enemy of the Jewish people. Yet, Jesus pointed out that the Samaritan was the one who followed the Greatest Commandment to love your neighbor. That cultural tidbit about the Samaritan helps us understand the parable's significance.

Reading Acts (New Testament Narrative)

Acts is a New Testament narrative written by Luke. It records the activities of the early church and bridges the gap between the four Gospels and the Epistles, the New Testament letters. Acts is known by many as "Acts of the Holy Spirit through the apostles." That's because Acts shows us how the Holy Spirit works in his people to continue Jesus's ministry of moving the gospel forward.

As you read the book of Acts, pay attention to the Holy Spirit's work in the lives of believers. Acts gives us examples to live by. So, instead of saying, "Do this and do that," Acts *shows* Christians how to be empowered and guided by the Holy Spirit to do God's work.

For a passage to serve as an example for us today, the subject should be: 1) clearly and consistently taught in the New Testament, and 2) be a part of the early churches' New Testament core beliefs and routine practices. This includes moral truths, water baptisms, and taking communion.

Reading the Letters (Epistles)

The New Testament letters (called Epistles) were written by apostles or someone who was close to them. These letters were considered to be authoritative because they were written by those who saw Jesus alive after he rose from the dead. Most of the New Testament was written by Paul. Other biblical writers include Peter, James, John, Jude, and the unknown author of Hebrews.

These letters were written to a specific church body or person to let them know how to handle a specific situation. The New Testament letters include stern warnings, explanations of prior teachings, corrections of false teachings, and explain the teachings of Jesus more in-depth. As for the layout, the New Testament letters are comparable to a formally typed letter, with an opening, a body, and a closing.

To understand a New Testament letter, it's helpful to know what problem the church body or person was facing. It's also good to read an entire letter in one sitting. This is how they were initially read. If you're not able to read the letter all at once, just know how the passage you're reading fits in with the rest of the letter.

Hearing God through the New Testament

The New Testament is filled with guidance, promises, and hope for the future. As you read the New Testament, make sure you read enough Scripture at once to really understand the point of the passage. Ask yourself, "What is the point of this passage?" and "How would God want me to apply the point, the timeless message, to my life today?"

Chapter 8 Journaling Activity

Read John 14:12–14 and prayerfully go through these steps, connecting with God through the passages:

K — Know the story behind the Bible book you're reading from (historical-cultural context).

The Bible book's background may include the who, what, when, where and why of the book. The Bible book's purpose (the story behind the Bible book) can be found in the scripture itself, a Bible handbook, background commentary, or your personal Bible may have it in the Bible book's introduction.

Write out the purpose for the book (the book's background information).

_____

_____

_____

_____

_____

I — Identify the overall message — a section of Scripture at a time (literary context).

Read through the section of Scripture your passage is found in to get a feel for the big picture, the overall message. Then, ask yourself what one word or phrase sums up the overall message. A section can include a chapter or so, such as in Psalms, or an entire book, such as in Philemon. Read the passage in light of the Bible book's purpose.

Jot down one word, phrase, or sentence that sums up the overall message of the section.

_____

_____

_____

_____

_____

N—Notice what a passage says and the details that stand out to you one paragraph at a time:

Information you may want to notice includes: Repeated words (keywords); commands; warnings/consequences; promises; conditional clauses; purpose statements (in order that, so that, etc.); verbs; figurative language/descriptive language; dialogue/conversations; examples (both negative and positive); truths; explanations.

Jot down the main point for each paragraph (or smaller portion of scripture) within the section you are studying. Then, write down the details that stand out to you. You may want to write down unfamiliar words along with their definitions.

_____

_____

_____

_____

_____

G—Grasp the message given to the original recipients:

After looking over steps 1–3, summarize the biblical author's message to the original recipients; what specifically did the author want them to do, believe, or understand?

Write out a past-tense statement that summarizes what the author wanted the original recipients to do, believe, or understand specifically.

_____

_____

_____

_____

_____

S—Seek the timeless truths:

A passage or command is timeless if it: 1) reveals God's character or how to live according to his ways or 2) includes moral truths and/or specific commands that are consistently taught and supported throughout Scripture, especially in the New Testament and 3) can be applied today by anyone from anywhere. (A passage may also reveal something about human nature, the church, etc.)

Write down God's timeless message and truths revealed in the passage.

_____

_____

_____

_____

_____

!—Apply God's word to your life:

Reflecting on the timeless message and truths, ask God to show you how to personally apply the truths to your life. Be still and wait for God to reveal how he wants you to respond to his Word.

Journal how God is leading you to apply the passage to your heart, mind, attitude, and life decisions.

_____

_____

_____

_____

_____

PART 4

Developing a Spirit-led Lifestyle

Chapter 9

WORDS OF POWER

YES! FINALLY! AFTER YEARS and years of earnestly praying, God had *finally* answered a specific prayer request of mine. I couldn't wait to share the news with my hubby! So, I sent him a text, pouring out my heart and soul. Every ounce of my being was sent through that message. I kept my phone close by me, anticipating the moment he would respond. When I heard my phone buzz, I rushed to open the message. There it was—his response: A thumbs up. A plain. Old. Thumbs. Up.

Looking at his response, I thought, *Really? That's the reply I get after I bore my soul in that text message? A thumbs up?* Though I laugh about it now, in that moment I felt quite frustrated. That was not exactly the response I was looking for from my Prince Charming!

Likewise, God also sends us his text, pouring out his heart and soul. His text, in essence, is God himself (John 1:1). The Bible lines up with the very person of Jesus Christ! It's not just a book written by talented authors. It's God's heart, his will, his plans, his guidance, his wisdom, and even his power. Power to do his will in his strength!

Without thinking, many people, even Christians, will disobey it. But, when they do, they are disobeying God himself. Others minimize the truth and power of God's Word. In reality, they're not denying an outdated book, they're denying God.

The Bible is a personal love letter to us from our Creator, so he doesn't want some meaningless thumbs up from us or a half-hearted, "I do." He, too, desires a wholehearted response and a steadfast commitment. You see, if we respond to God's Word in love and obedience, it will transform our very nature.

God's Word Transforms Us

God's Word transforms our very being. In fact, we're not created to walk according to our desires, our ability, or our flesh—we are to walk and live in his nature, which is: *love, joy, peace, patience, kindness, goodness, faithfulness, gentleness and self-control* (Galatians 5:22–23). To do this, we need his power as it works through his Word.

Let's be honest, it's easy to allow our busy lives and hectic schedules to get in the way of reading God's Word. But, when we don't spend time with God, we become spiritually weak. Then, we end up addicted to—and enslaved to—the things of this world: wealth, material possessions, sports, sex, food, and other things. And, day after day, we'll end up giving in to our self-destructive ways.

You see, we can't fight spiritual battles in our own strength (Ephesians 6:12–13). We'll give up. We'll lose. We need God's supernatural wisdom, guidance, and strength. And we can only receive his power by spending time in his presence through his Word and persistent prayer.

In reality, meditating on God's Word and spending time with him causes our sinful nature to peel away. That's why we need to read the Bible even when we don't feel like it. Sure, we may begin reading the Bible feeling tired, emotionally drained, and spiritually weak. But, if we'll faithfully read it, no matter how we're feeling, we will overcome our areas of weakness.

Hebrews 4:12 (HCSB) testifies, "For the word of God is living and effective and sharper than any two-edged sword, penetrating as far as the separation of soul and spirit, joints and marrow. It is able to judge the ideas and thoughts of the heart."

God's Word has the power to reshape your thoughts, beliefs, actions, attitudes, and choices so you can fulfill your God-given mission.

Created for a Purpose

God created us to love and serve him. And, when God becomes our first love, we'll fulfill our life's mission, because God forms his purposes in us and his desires become our desires. So, we can trust, in his timing, he will open doors of opportunities for us to serve him. He will also provide ways for us to use the talents and abilities he's given us for his glory. God's Word will give us the power to be all he created us to be.

Philippians 2:13 (NLT) reaffirms this truth: "God is working in you, giving you the desire and the power to do what pleases him."

To live out our God-given purpose, we must live according to God's power. This means we must:

Prioritize reading the Bible and spending time in prayer. We need to plan when and where we'll spend quality time connecting with God. Otherwise, it will end up at the bottom of our to-do lists. Casually reading bits and pieces of the Bible will not help us overcome carnal desires, attitudes, and actions.

Start the day with God. If at all possible, spend time with God in the morning. This will help you see everything from his eternal perspective. You'll be reminded that God has your life (and the world's affairs) in his hands under his sovereign control.

Psalm 143:8 (NIV) reminds us of this truth: "Let the morning bring me word of your unfailing love, for I have put my trust in you. Show me the way I should go, for to you I entrust my life."

Meditate on God's Word throughout the day. Also, make it a habit of thinking on God's Word throughout the day. No need to make this hard. Simply choose a few passages to focus on or use the passages that stood out to you during your morning devotions. Then, take a few minutes during lunch and before bed to reflect on them. Starting this small routine has the potential to make a huge impact in your life!

Psalm 92:2 (NLT) says, "It is good to proclaim your unfailing love in the morning, your faithfulness in the evening."

Communicate with God through his Word. As you read the Bible, focus on the passages that stir your heart. In response to those passages, you might feel led to communicate with God through praise and worship, giving thanks, repenting from sins, or sitting quietly in his presence in awe and wonder of who he is. Also, pray God's Word back to him, especially the passages that catch your attention.

Obey God's Word from the Inside Out. If we love God, we will want to please him with our heart, mind, attitude, actions, and choices. So, obey what God's Word plainly teaches, and obey what the Holy Spirit is speaking to you personally through the passages.

First John 2:3–6 (HCSB) says, "This is how we are sure that we have come to know Him; by keeping His commands. The one who says, 'I have come to know Him,' yet doesn't keep His commands, is a liar, and the truth is not in him. But whoever keeps His word, truly in him the love of God is perfected. This is how we know we are in Him; the one who says he remains in Him should walk just as He walked."

Salvation is not based on what we do. But, when we don't obey God, we're living outside the will and blessing of God. Though our flesh is weak, God's Word is powerful and enables us to obey him—if we spend quality time with God. For this to happen, we must be willing to receive his love, guidance, correction, warning, and forgiveness.

Now, let me encourage anyone who struggles with a particular sin. If you struggle with your thought life or an addiction of any kind, know that you cannot overcome these addictions in your own strength. Instead, keep reading and meditating on God's Word—even while you're struggling with the same sin. Remember, God is working in you through his Word to give you the desire and the power to do what pleases him (Philippians 2:13). Also, for support, I'd encourage you to find a trusted Christian leader, counselor, or support group to meet with regularly. That way you'll have help when you feel tempted to give up.

It's spiritually vital for you to persevere in God's Word—no matter how long it takes. Don't let your sin stop you from praying and reading God's Word; In reality, reading God's Word and praying help keep you from sin. If you consistently spend time with God and read his Word, it will continue to work in you and change your heart, mind, and actions.

Guard your heart. We must guard our hearts against attitudes and actions that don't line up with Scripture. Also, it's important that we deliberately draw closer to God. Don't be passive with what you watch, hear, say, or do! Be alert!

Be careful not to spend hours passively entertaining yourself with movies, YouTube clips, shows, songs, video/computer games or anything else. This will cause you to become preoccupied with the things of this world. Even too much of a good or acceptable thing distracts us from the life God has for us. Without realizing it, our love for God will fade and sin will reside in our hearts, diminishing God's influence and power in our lives.

God is holy, holy, holy. For that reason, *anything* that hinders our relationship with God needs to be removed from our lives. For example, we cannot expect to watch movies, or any other form of entertainment, that places ungodly images in our minds (such as violence, nudity, or filthy language, etc.) and be close to God. That's because it will grieve the Holy Spirit (God's presence in our lives). So, remember to guard your heart, my friend!

First Peter 5:8 (AMP) warns, "Be sober [well balanced and self-disciplined], be alert *and* cautious at all times. That enemy of yours, the devil, prowls around like a roaring lion [fiercely hungry], seeking someone to devour."

Moving Forward in Love and Power

Loving God is a lifestyle, affecting the outcome and our approach to every area of our lives. This doesn't make life easy, it makes life purposeful.

Prayerfully reading and obeying God's Word will reshape our hearts' desires, what we think about, what we do, the attitudes we have, and the choices we make. But we need to read and engage in God's Word consistently. We need to be committed and purposeful in our pursuit of God. God loves you deeply and created you with a special purpose in mind. Allow him to fulfill his purpose in you by his power that is readily available through his Word.

My Personal Devotional Habits

I'd like to finish this Bible-reading guide by sharing my personal devotional habits that help me have an intimate relationship with God.

First, here are some attitudes and approaches
I apply when reading Scripture:

- *I spend alone time with God in the morning.* Though it's not always the very first thing I do, I pray and read my Bible before my crazy day begins. This helps me be spiritually stronger throughout the day, so I can walk according to God's will and overcome temptation.

- *Prayer is about expressing my love to God and receiving his love and grace for me.* If I look at prayer as something just to do, I find that it becomes burdensome. Spending time with God is truly a joy and blessing.

- *I take time to connect with God, not just communicate to him.* Usually, I spend about an hour with the Lord, reading his Word and praying. Although an hour may seem like a long time, the point is I don't want to feel hurried during my time with him. The amount of time isn't what truly matters. The important thing is to take enough time to genuinely connect with God through Scripture and prayer.

- *I allow the Holy Spirit to energize my prayers.* Often, I start my devotional time by sitting quietly in God's presence for a few minutes. Then, I begin communicating with him by allowing the Holy Spirit to energize (e.g., lead) my prayers (usually by praying Scripture or worshipping God). I communicate with God by giving him praise and worship, expressing thanks, repenting from sins, or sitting quietly in awe and wonder of who he is. Also, I pray the scriptures back to God.

Overall, the framework for how I pray (e.g., verbally communicate my love for God) is inspired by the prayer that Jesus models in Matthew 6:9–13:

- *I give God my cares and anxieties and trust him to help me.* When my mind is distracted by the things and anxieties of this world, I cannot focus on God or enjoy his presence. So, I may start by praying something like, "God, I am worried about (the specific situations/circumstances). So, Jesus, I give these cares to you and trust you to help me. Thank you, God, for taking care of _____. You are so good!" I do not talk or vent about these problems to God. Instead, I give each of my burdens to God in prayer and then let go of them.

- *Praise and Worship*: Next, I often start worshipping God, because I find that it energizes the rest of my time with him. As I worship God for who he is, his presence ignites my heart and mind. Sometimes I will just sing spontaneously as it flows from my heart and mind. Other times, I sing certain verses of Scripture, or even just a simple worship song that I know of, such as "I Love You, Lord."

- *Give Thanks:* After praise and worship, I flow right into giving God thanks for who he is and all he's done. I thank him specifically for answered prayers.

- *Repent:* After giving God thanks, I ask God to forgive me for specific sins I've committed. I also ask the Holy Spirit to show me sins that I'm blind to. As the Holy Spirit reveals these areas (that I've lived contrary to his will and ways), I repent from them. I'll also ask God, and trust him, to help me overcome specific areas of weakness and temptation in my life. Then, I thank God for forgiving me.

- *Prayer Requests:* Next, I humbly, yet boldly, ask God to provide for all my specific requests. When I pray for my spiritual, physical, and emotional needs, I put confidence in God's goodness and sovereignty to meet them. I thank him in advance for answering my prayers. Likewise, I ask for whatever I believe the Holy Spirit is leading me to pray for, because I know the Holy Spirit always leads me to pray God's will. Also, I may ask God for something I want (not necessarily need), but I leave it up to God for how to meet those requests. I do not "name it and claim it." Instead, I give God my wants and trust him to ultimately do what's eternally best.

- *Devotional Bible Reading and Listening:* Then, using the P-R-A-Y Method, I meditate on God's Word and "listen" to him through Scripture. After that, I take time to sit quietly in God's presence to see if he puts something else on my heart. Usually, I end my devotional time by asking God if there's anything he wants me to do that day. At that point, I will wait to see if God puts something specific on my heart to do, such as contacting someone.

Devotional Bible reading can be done at any point in one's prayer time. Some people prefer to read their Bible first. Personally, I read it towards the end of my devotional time. When using the Bible as a devotional, please know that Scripture still needs to be read in context.

Also, I continue to mediate on God's Word throughout the day. I do this by taking a few minutes during lunch and before bed to reflect on Scripture. Most often, I use the passages that stand out to me during my morning devotions. Or, I'll pick a particular verse to help me overcome a specific area of temptation in my life. For example, I often fight thoughts of depression, so I will choose a verse that fills me with hope.

To guard my heart against temptation, I make sure these scriptures are available for me to read and pray all the time. That's why I either jot the verse down on a note or have my Bible open to the passage. The point is, I *purposefully* meditate on God's Word throughout the day to keep my thinking in line with God's truth.

My Prayer for You

These practices have truly changed my life, but please know that everyone's prayer time will be unique. Most importantly, remember to communicate with God and connect with him each day. To live out your God-given potential and purpose, you'll need to consistently read and apply God's Word to your heart, mind, actions, attitudes, and words. My prayer is that you'll know God's truth and experience his presence, power, and purpose in your life.

Chapter 9 Journaling Activity

Read Luke 8:4–15: In the parable of the seeds, Jesus describes four different types of soil.

The first soil includes the seed that fell along the road. What happens to this seed (v. 12)? How do you think the devil takes away the Word from people's hearts?

_____

_____

_____

_____

_____

The second soil includes the seed that fell among the rock. According to this passage, what causes them to fall away (v. 13)? Why do you think this group of people falls away when trials come while others don't?

_____

_____

_____

_____

_____

The third soil includes seed that fell among the thorns. This soil was harmed by anxiety, worldly pleasures, and the cares of this life. How do you think anxiety, worldly pleasures, and the cares of this life affect our relationship with God? How have anxiety and the pleasures of this world affected your relationship with God personally?

_____

_____

_____

_____

_____

What happened to the seed planted in the good soil (the fourth soil)?

_____

_____

_____

_____

What do you think the difference is between the three hindered soils and the fourth soil? What things can you do specifically to persevere in your walk with God?

_____

_____

_____

_____

_____

PART 5

Bible Tools and Quick Reference Guides

MEET-ME-HERE JOURNEY INSTRUCTIONS

GROWING IN OUR RELATIONSHIP with God takes preparation and dedication. The meet-Me-here Journey is a 40-day devotional kickoff. This journey is to help you develop devotional habits so you will experience God's presence, walk in his power, and live out your God-given purpose. During this journey, you will spend time with God in prayer and Bible reading each day. Then, once a week, meet with a trusted friend, group, or our online community, to receive support through meaningful conversations and weekly check-ins. This program is for churches, groups, and individuals.

How This Journey Works:

- Initially, you or your group will need to decide on a Bible-reading plan. If you'd like, there is an optional plan in the Progress Journal. Or, you or your group may decide that everyone will choose their own Scripture to read daily.

- Then, if you haven't already, find a church group, trusted mentor, or an accountability partner to support you. (If you'd like, I often offer a 40-day accountability program for a low cost at www.kim-christine.com.)

- Each day (preferably in the morning), spend time connecting with God through prayer and Bible reading. We suggest you prayerfully read one chapter a day (or more if you wish). You can keep track of your time using the 40-day Accountability Journal in this book.

- Once a week, meet with a trusted friend or group. During the meetings, encourage one another and have each person answer the conversation questions below. After each person has responded to the questions, pray for one another.

  - **First Session Conversation Questions:** For the first meeting, the leader or accountability partner asks each person these two questions: 1) What practical choices do you need to make today to grow closer to God? (Or, to prioritize God, what is one thing you should start or stop doing?) 2) How can I/we pray for you?

  - **Conversation Questions:** For each remaining session, the leader or accountability partner asks each person these questions: 1) How are you doing with your 40-day devotional journey? (Helpful prompts: Did you connect with God through prayer and Bible reading throughout last week? If so, how did spending time with God influence your daily choices?) 2) What did God show you about himself through his Word this week? 3) How can I/we pray for you?

  - **Close in Prayer**

Although it's your responsibility to follow through with the daily devotional practices, your spiritual mentor should support you. You are not in this alone!

MEET-ME-HERE JOURNEY SPIRITUAL PLANNER

1. Decide on a Bible Reading Plan: What reading plan will you follow?

2. Find an accountability partner or group: Who will hold you accountable and offer you encouragement on a weekly basis?

3. Decide when and where you will daily spend time with God: When and where will you regularly spend time with God?

4. Choose a time and place to meet with your accountability group or partner on a weekly basis. Where and when will you meet with your accountability group/leader?

40-DAY PROGRESS JOURNAL & BIBLE READING OPTIONS

Day 1: Date: _____

- ☐ Spent time in prayer: Praise & Worship, Thanksgiving, Repentance, and Petitions
- ☐ Read Bible. Scripture: _____
- ☐ Meditated on verse: _____
- ☐ Bible journaling/other: _____
  - Bible Reading Options: NT: John 1:1–18; Wisdom: Ecclesiastes 3:1–8; OT: Genesis 1; History: 1 Chronicles 1

Day 2: Date: _____

- ☐ Spent time in prayer: Praise & Worship, Thanksgiving, Repentance, and Petitions
- ☐ Read Bible. Scripture: _____
- ☐ Meditated on verse: _____
- ☐ Bible journaling/other: _____
  - Bible Reading Options: NT: John 1:19–51; Wisdom: Psalm 1; OT: Genesis 2; History: 1 Chronicles 2

Day 3: Date: _____

- ☐ Spent time in prayer: Praise & Worship, Thanksgiving, Repentance, and Petitions
- ☐ Read Bible. Scripture: _____
- ☐ Meditated on verse: _____
- ☐ Bible journaling/other: _____

    - Bible Reading Options: NT: John 2; Wisdom: Psalm 2; OT: Genesis 3; History: 1 Chronicles 3

Day 4: Date: _____

- ☐ Spent time in prayer: Praise & Worship, Thanksgiving, Repentance, and Petitions
- ☐ Read Bible. Scripture: _____
- ☐ Meditated on verse: _____
- ☐ Bible journaling/other: _____

    - Bible Reading Options: NT: John 3:1–21; Wisdom: Psalm 3; OT: Genesis 4; History: 1 Chronicles 4

Day 5: Date: _____

- ☐ Spent time in prayer: Praise & Worship, Thanksgiving, Repentance, and Petitions
- ☐ Read Bible. Scripture: _____
- ☐ Meditated on verse: _____
- ☐ Bible journaling/other: _____

    - Bible Reading Options: NT: John 3:22–36; Wisdom: Psalm 4; OT: Genesis 5; History: 1 Chronicles 5

Day 6: Date: _____

- ☐ Spent time in prayer: Praise & Worship, Thanksgiving, Repentance, and Petitions
- ☐ Read Bible. Scripture: _____
- ☐ Meditated on verse: _____
- ☐ Bible journaling/other: _____

  - Bible Reading Options: NT: John 4:1–42; Wisdom: Psalm 5; OT: Genesis 6; History: 1 Chronicles 6

Day 7: Date: _____

- ☐ Spent time in prayer: Praise & Worship, Thanksgiving, Repentance, and Petitions
- ☐ Read Bible. Scripture: _____
- ☐ Meditated on verse: _____
- ☐ Bible journaling/other: _____

  - Bible Reading Options: NT: John 4:43—5:18; Wisdom: Psalm 6; OT: Genesis 7; History: 1 Chronicles 7

Day 8: Date: _____

- ☐ Spent time in prayer: Praise & Worship, Thanksgiving, Repentance, and Petitions
- ☐ Read Bible. Scripture: _____
- ☐ Meditated on verse: _____
- ☐ Bible journaling/other: _____

  - Bible Reading Options: NT: John 5:19–47; Wisdom: Psalm 7; OT: Genesis 8:1–19; History: 1 Chronicles 8

Day 9: Date: _____

- ☐ Spent time in prayer: Praise & Worship, Thanksgiving, Repentance, and Petitions
- ☐ Read Bible. Scripture: _____
- ☐ Meditated on verse: _____
- ☐ Bible journaling/other: _____

  - Bible Reading Options: NT: John 6:1–21; Wisdom: Psalm 8; OT: Genesis 8:20—9:19; History: 1 Chronicles 9

Day 10: Date: _____

- ☐ Spent time in prayer: Praise & Worship, Thanksgiving, Repentance, and Petitions
- ☐ Read Bible. Scripture: _____
- ☐ Meditated on verse: _____
- ☐ Bible journaling/other: _____

  - Bible Reading Options: NT: John 6:22–71; Wisdom: Psalm 9; OT: Genesis 9:20—10:32; History: 1 Chronicles 10

Day 11: Date: _____

- ☐ Spent time in prayer: Praise & Worship, Thanksgiving, Repentance, and Petitions
- ☐ Read Bible. Scripture: _____
- ☐ Meditated on verse: _____
- ☐ Bible journaling/other: _____

  - Bible Reading Options: NT: John 7; Wisdom: Psalm 10; OT: Genesis 11; History: 1 Chronicles 11

Day 12: Date: _____

- ☐ Spent time in prayer: Praise & Worship, Thanksgiving, Repentance, and Petitions
- ☐ Read Bible. Scripture: _____
- ☐ Meditated on verse: _____
- ☐ Bible journaling/other: _____

  - Bible Reading Options: NT: John 8; Wisdom: Psalm 11; OT: Genesis 12—13:1; History: 1 Chronicles 12

Day 13: Date: _____

- ☐ Spent time in prayer: Praise & Worship, Thanksgiving, Repentance, and Petitions
- ☐ Read Bible. Scripture: _____
- ☐ Meditated on verse: _____
- ☐ Bible journaling/other: _____

  - Bible Reading Options: NT: John 9; Wisdom: Psalm 12; OT: Genesis 13:2–18; History: 1 Chronicles 13

Day 14: Date: _____

- ☐ Spent time in prayer: Praise & Worship, Thanksgiving, Repentance, and Petitions
- ☐ Read Bible. Scripture: _____
- ☐ Meditated on verse: _____
- ☐ Bible journaling/other: _____

  - Bible Reading Options: NT: John 10:1–18; Wisdom: Psalm 13; OT: Genesis 14; History: 1 Chronicles 14

Day 15: Date: _____

- ☐ Spent time in prayer: Praise & Worship, Thanksgiving, Repentance, and Petitions
- ☐ Read Bible. Scripture: _____
- ☐ Meditated on verse: _____
- ☐ Bible journaling/other: _____

  - Bible Reading Options: NT: John 10:19–42; Wisdom: Psalm 14; OT: Genesis 15; History: 1 Chronicles 15:1—16: 3

Day 16: Date: _____

- ☐ Spent time in prayer: Praise & Worship, Thanksgiving, Repentance, and Petitions
- ☐ Read Bible. Scripture: _____
- ☐ Meditated on verse: _____
- ☐ Bible journaling/other: _____

  - Bible Reading Options: NT: John 11:1–54; Wisdom: Psalm 15; OT: Genesis 16; History: 1 Chronicles 16:4–43

Day 17: Date: _____

- ☐ Spent time in prayer: Praise & Worship, Thanksgiving, Repentance, and Petitions
- ☐ Read Bible. Scripture: _____
- ☐ Meditated on verse: _____
- ☐ Bible journaling/other: _____

  - Bible Reading Options: NT: John 11:55—12:19; Wisdom: Psalm 16; OT: Genesis 17; History: 1 Chronicles 17

Day 18: Date: _____

☐ Spent time in prayer: Praise & Worship, Thanksgiving, Repentance, and Petitions

☐ Read Bible. Scripture: _____

☐ Meditated on verse: _____

☐ Bible journaling/other: _____

- Bible Reading Options: NT: John 12:20–50; Wisdom: Psalm 17; OT: Genesis 18:1–15; History: 1 Chronicles 18—20

Day 19: Date: _____

☐ Spent time in prayer: Praise & Worship, Thanksgiving, Repentance, and Petitions

☐ Read Bible. Scripture: _____

☐ Meditated on verse: _____

☐ Bible journaling/other: _____

- Bible Reading Options: NT: John 13; Wisdom: Psalm 18; OT: Genesis 18:16–33; History: 1 Chronicles 21:1–17

Day 20: Date: _____

☐ Spent time in prayer: Praise & Worship, Thanksgiving, Repentance, and Petitions

☐ Read Bible. Scripture: _____

☐ Meditated on verse: _____

☐ Bible journaling/other: _____

- Bible Reading Options: NT: John 14; Wisdom: Psalm 19; OT: Genesis 19; History: 1 Chronicles 21:18—22:19

Day 21: Date: _____

☐ Spent time in prayer: Praise & Worship, Thanksgiving, Repentance, and Petitions

☐ Read Bible. Scripture: _____

☐ Meditated on verse: _____

☐ Bible journaling/other: _____

- Bible Reading Options: NT: John 15:1–17; Wisdom: Psalm 20; OT: Genesis 20; History: 1 Chronicles 23—24

Day 22: Date: _____

☐ Spent time in prayer: Praise & Worship, Thanksgiving, Repentance, and Petitions

☐ Read Bible. Scripture: _____

☐ Meditated on verse: _____

☐ Bible journaling/other: _____

- Bible Reading Options: NT: John 15:18—16:15; Wisdom: Psalm 21; OT: Genesis 21:1–21; History: 1 Chronicles 25

Day 23: Date: _____

☐ Spent time in prayer: Praise & Worship, Thanksgiving, Repentance, and Petitions

☐ Read Bible. Scripture: _____

☐ Meditated on verse: _____

☐ Bible journaling/other: _____

- Bible Reading Options: NT: John 16:16–33; Wisdom: Psalm 22; OT: Genesis 21:22–34; History: 1 Chronicles 26

Day 24: Date: _____

☐ Spent time in prayer: Praise & Worship, Thanksgiving, Repentance, and Petitions

☐ Read Bible. Scripture: _____

☐ Meditated on verse: _____

☐ Bible journaling/other: _____

- Bible Reading Options: NT: John 17; Wisdom: Psalm 23; OT: Genesis 22; History: 1 Chronicles 27

Day 25: Date: _____

☐ Spent time in prayer: Praise & Worship, Thanksgiving, Repentance, and Petitions

☐ Read Bible. Scripture: _____

☐ Meditated on verse: _____

☐ Bible journaling/other: _____

- Bible Reading Options: NT: John 18:1–27; Wisdom: Psalm 24; OT: Genesis 23; History: 1 Chronicles 28

Day 26: Date: _____

☐ Spent time in prayer: Praise & Worship, Thanksgiving, Repentance, and Petitions

☐ Read Bible. Scripture: _____

☐ Meditated on verse: _____

☐ Bible journaling/other: _____

- Bible Reading Options: NT: John 18:28—19:16; Wisdom: Psalm 25; OT: Genesis 24; History: 1 Chronicles 29:1–22a

Day 27: Date: _____

☐ Spent time in prayer: Praise & Worship, Thanksgiving, Repentance, and Petitions

☐ Read Bible. Scripture: _____

☐ Meditated on verse: _____

☐ Bible journaling/other: _____

- Bible Reading Options: NT: John 19:17–42; Wisdom: Psalm 26; OT: Genesis 25:1–18; History: 1 Chronicles 29:22b–30

Day 28: Date: _____

☐ Spent time in prayer: Praise & Worship, Thanksgiving, Repentance, and Petitions

☐ Read Bible. Scripture: _____

☐ Meditated on verse: _____

☐ Bible journaling/other: _____

- Bible Reading Options: NT: John 20; Wisdom: Psalm 27; OT: Genesis 25:19–34; History: 2 Chronicles 1

Day 29: Date: _____

☐ Spent time in prayer: Praise & Worship, Thanksgiving, Repentance, and Petitions

☐ Read Bible. Scripture: _____

☐ Meditated on verse: _____

☐ Bible journaling/other: _____

- Bible Reading Options: NT: John 21; Wisdom: Psalm 28; OT: Genesis 26; History: 2 Chronicles 2

Day 30: Date: _____

- ☐ Spent time in prayer: Praise & Worship, Thanksgiving, Repentance, and Petitions
- ☐ Read Bible. Scripture: _____
- ☐ Meditated on verse: _____
- ☐ Bible journaling/other: _____

   • Bible Reading Options: NT: Romans 1:1–17; Wisdom: Psalm 29; OT: Genesis 27:1–40; History: 2 Chronicles 3

Day 31: Date: _____

- ☐ Spent time in prayer: Praise & Worship, Thanksgiving, Repentance, and Petitions
- ☐ Read Bible. Scripture: _____
- ☐ Meditated on verse: _____
- ☐ Bible journaling/other: _____

   • Bible Reading Options: NT: Romans 1:18–32; Wisdom: Psalm 30; OT: Genesis 27:41—28:9; History: 2 Chronicles 4

Day 32: Date: _____

- ☐ Spent time in prayer: Praise & Worship, Thanksgiving, Repentance, and Petitions
- ☐ Read Bible. Scripture: _____
- ☐ Meditated on verse: _____
- ☐ Bible journaling/other: _____

   • Bible Reading Options: NT: Romans 2:1–16; Wisdom: Psalm 31; OT: Genesis 28:10–22; History: 2 Chronicles 5

Day 33: Date: _____

☐ Spent time in prayer: Praise & Worship, Thanksgiving, Repentance, and Petitions

☐ Read Bible. Scripture: _____

☐ Meditated on verse: _____

☐ Bible journaling/other: _____

- Bible Reading Options: NT: Romans 2:17—3:8; Wisdom: Psalm 32; OT: Genesis 29:1–30; History: 2 Chronicles 6

Day 34: Date: _____

☐ Spent time in prayer: Praise & Worship, Thanksgiving, Repentance, and Petitions

☐ Read Bible. Scripture: _____

☐ Meditated on verse: _____

☐ Bible journaling/other: _____

- Bible Reading Options: NT: Romans 3:9–20; Wisdom: Psalm 33; OT: Genesis 29:31—30:43; History: 2 Chronicles 7

Day 35: Date: _____

☐ Spent time in prayer: Praise & Worship, Thanksgiving, Repentance, and Petitions

☐ Read Bible. Scripture: _____

☐ Meditated on verse: _____

☐ Bible journaling/other: _____

- Bible Reading Options: NT: Romans 3:21–31; Wisdom: Psalm 34; OT: Genesis 31 History: 2 Chronicles 8

Day 36: Date: _____

☐ Spent time in prayer: Praise & Worship, Thanksgiving, Repentance, and Petitions

☐ Read Bible. Scripture: _____

☐ Meditated on verse: _____

☐ Bible journaling/other: _____

- Bible Reading Options: NT: Romans 4; Wisdom: Psalm 35; OT: Genesis 32; History: 2 Chronicles 9

Day 37: Date: _____

☐ Spent time in prayer: Praise & Worship, Thanksgiving, Repentance, and Petitions

☐ Read Bible. Scripture: _____

☐ Meditated on verse: _____

☐ Bible journaling/other: _____

- Bible Reading Options: NT: Romans 5:1–11; Wisdom: Psalm 36; OT: Genesis 33; History: 2 Chronicles 10

Day 38: Date: _____

☐ Spent time in prayer: Praise & Worship, Thanksgiving, Repentance, and Petitions

☐ Read Bible. Scripture: _____

☐ Meditated on verse: _____

☐ Bible journaling/other: _____

- Bible Reading Options: NT: Romans 5:12–21; Wisdom: Psalm 37; OT: Genesis 34; History: 2 Chronicles 11

Day 39: Date: _____

- ☐ Spent time in prayer: Praise & Worship, Thanksgiving, Repentance, and Petitions
- ☐ Read Bible. Scripture: _____
- ☐ Meditated on verse: _____
- ☐ Bible journaling/other: _____

  - Bible Reading Options: NT: Romans 6; Wisdom: Psalm 38; OT: Genesis 35; History: 2 Chronicles 12

Day 40: Date: _____

- ☐ Spent time in prayer: Praise & Worship, Thanksgiving, Repentance, and Petitions
- ☐ Read Bible. Scripture: _____
- ☐ Meditated on verse: _____
- ☐ Bible journaling/other: _____

  - Bible Reading Options: NT: Romans 7; Wisdom: Psalm 39; OT: Genesis 36; History: 2 Chronicles 13

To continue with the Bible reading plan, you may visit kim-christine.com.

THE K-I-N-G-S-! QUICK REFERENCE GUIDE

Step 1: K—Know the purpose of the Bible book you're reading from (e.g., the historical-cultural context).

WHAT IS THE PURPOSE of the Bible book? To determine the Bible book's purpose (the story behind the Bible book you're reading from), find out why the biblical author wrote to the biblical audience. The book's purpose can be found in Scripture itself, a Bible handbook, background commentaries, or your personal Bible may have it in the Bible book's introduction. The Bible book's purpose may include the who, what, when, where, and why of the book.

Step 2: I—Identify the overall message within a section of Scripture (e.g., the literary context).
Read through an entire section of Scripture to get a feel for the overall message. Then, ask yourself what one word or phrase sums up the overall message. A section can include a chapter or so, such as in Psalms, or an entire book, such as in Philemon. Read the passage in light of the Bible book's purpose.

Step 3: N—Notice what a passage says and the details that stand out to you—one paragraph at a time:
Re-read the section of Scripture and notice what each paragraph actually says and the supporting details.

Examples of the type of details you may notice include: Repeated words (keywords), warnings, consequences, commands, promises, conditional words (If you see me, you will find me), words that show purpose (in order that; because; so that; so, etc.), subjects/ verbs, lists (example: Fruit of the Spirit, Galatians 5:22–23), examples and illustrations (Bible stories, etc.) dialogue, figures of speech, etc.

Step 4: G—Grasp the message given to the original recipients:
After looking over steps 1–3, summarize the biblical author's message to the original recipients; what specifically did the author want them to do, believe, or understand?

Step 5: S—Seek the timeless truths:
A passage or command is timeless if it: 1) reveals God's character or how to live according to his ways or 2) includes moral truths and/or specific commands that are consistently taught and supported throughout Scripture, especially in the New Testament and 3) can be applied today by anyone from anywhere. (A passage may also reveal something about human nature, the church, etc.) Identify the timeless message and truths revealed in the passage.

Step 6: !—Apply God's word to your life:
Reflecting on the timeless message and truths, ask God to show you how to personally apply the truths to your life. Be quiet before the Lord, and do not hurry through this step. Ask the Holy Spirit, "How do you want me to respond to your Word? What would you have me do?" Patiently wait for God to show you how to personally apply His message to your life. We must respond to God's Word with our entire being: heart, soul, mind, attitude, words, actions, and choices. Our response starts from the inside and should result in changed behavior, thoughts, actions, and attitudes.

THE P-R-A-Y QUICK REFERENCE GUIDE

AFTER SLOWLY READING THROUGH a complete section of Scripture, which is usually about a chapter or so, follow the P-R-A-Y Bible Reading Method below:

P—Passage: What *passage* of Scripture stand(s) out to you? Write down the passage(s) that stand(s) out to you.

R—Reveal: What does the passage *reveal* (especially about God and His ways)? A passage may also reveal something about human nature or the church. What timeless point does the passage reveal about God's will or ways? Write down what the passage reveals.

A—Ask: Come up with questions that will help you examine your heart, mind, attitudes, and life decisions in light of the passage. Jot down questions to ask that will help reflect on your life in view of the passage.

Y—Yield: How is God leading you to *yield* to the passage? What is the Holy Spirit revealing to you about your life in view of the passage? What is the Holy Spirit telling you to do specifically to apply the passage to your heart, mind, actions, and attitude? Journal how the Holy Spirit is leading you to personally respond to the passage.

THE 4-P QUICK REFERENCE GUIDE

P—Passage: After reading a whole section of Scripture at a time, write down the *passage* that catches your attention. A section can include a chapter or so, such as in Psalms, or an entire book, such as in Philemon.

P—Point: Write the timeless *point* God is making through the passage you wrote down. What is the point or the purpose of the passage? It may be helpful to look for words that reveal the "why" such as, because, so, for, etc. (If you prefer, you may choose to write down the overall point of the section you read.)

P—Personalize: Write how God is leading you to personally apply the passage. Ask God to show you how to *personally apply* the timeless message to your heart, mind, actions, attitudes, and lifestyle choices. Take time to really meditate on the passage and listen for how God is leading you to specifically apply the passage in your own life.

P—Pray: *Pray* the Scripture back to God, asking him to help you apply the Scripture to your heart, mind, and actions. As you pray through a passage, you may choose to pray it word for word, or personalize portions of the Scripture by inserting specific names or situations into it. Simply allow the Scripture to shape your prayers. Journal your prayer to God.